American Guide Series

CHILLICOTHE
AND ROSS COUNTY

The Old David B. Smart Home

American Guide Series

CHILLICOTHE
AND ROSS COUNTY

Compiled and Written by

FEDERAL WRITERS' PROJECT OF OHIO

Works Progress Administration

Sponsored by

The Ross County

NORTHWEST TERRITORY COMMITTEE

1938

In conjunction with Rotary, Kiwanis, Lions, Chamber of Commerce and the Junior Chamber of Commerce

COMMONWEALTH BOOK COMPANY
St. Martin, Ohio
2024

Copyright © 1938 by The Ross County Northwest Territory Committee
This edition copyright © 2024 by Commonwealth Book Company, Inc.

All rights reserved. No part of this book may be reproduced in any form or by any means without the prior written consent of the publisher, excepting brief quotes used in reviews. Printed in the United States of America.

ISBN: 978-1-948986-78-6

WORKS PROGRESS ADMINISTRATION

HARRY L. HOPKINS, *Administrator*

ELLEN S. WOODWARD, *Assistant Administrator*

HENRY G. ALSBERG, *Director of Federal Writers Project*

COVER IMAGE: POSTCARD VIEW OF CHILLICOTHE, CIRCA 1930

PREFACE

Chillicothe is an old and full-flavored Ohio town, and Ross County has stamped its image on the great seal of the State. This book tells the story in words and pictures of this first capitol of Ohio. All the work has been done by the Federal Writers' Project of the Works Progress Administration in Ohio; by its research staff, typists, writers, and editors.

Everybody now knows the story of how these Projects were organized to give honorable aid to professional people whom the long depression has robbed of their jobs. More than a hundred workers are employed on the Writers' Project in this State. They have gone through old newspapers, private journals and scrapbooks, neglected archives, and they have had personal interviews with informed citizens. From these sources, some of which might easily have been lost to posterity, they have got together the story of the past.

Ohio has never cultivated her legends so intensively as some of her good neighbors, but her history has been fairly long and lively. We hope that the work of the Writers' Project may help to re-awaken an active interest in this heritage, and stimulate creative talent to give it life. This work on Chillicothe and Ross County, a part of the American Guide Series, is one of several forthcoming publications on Ohio.

HARLAN HATCHER, *State Director.*

ON THE USE OF THE BOOK

This book is an informal guide to Chillicothe and Ross County.

A section on *General Information* offers guidance on practical matters for Chillicothe visitors.

The body of the *Guide* tells about the past and present of Chillicothe, with essays on its history, society, politics, industry, customs, art, architecture, letters, theatre, and the press.

The *Tour Section* is designed to guide the visitor to the points of interest about the town. These points are numbered in the text to correspond with key numbers spotted on the city map for convenient location. A list of the more interesting old houses with a brief description of each has been included.

The second part of the *Guide* gives an account of Ross County with essays on geology, archæology, agriculture and other subjects. The towns and villages are described briefly in alphabetical order. A *Tour of the County,* with points of interest numbered in the text to correspond with the numbers on the county map, is included, together with directions and mileage from Chillicothe.

The photographs have been selected to give the reader a quick visual comprehension of this diversified city and county. Because Chillicothe is noted for its Greek Revival homes, several pictures of houses have been included.

CONTENTS

Preface
    By Harlan Hatcher, State Director, Federal Writers' Project............ 5
On the Use of the Book... 6
General Information 8
Chillicothe Today 9
The Founding of a City and a State... 10
Waterways and Turnpikes... 15
Canal Days and the Railroad Era.. 17
Industry; Past and Present... 22
Customs, Manners, Social Life... 25
Chillicothe Citizens and Where They Came From... 32
Chillicothe and the Wars... 34
"Knowledge Being Necessary to Good Government"....................................... 39
The Press 40
The Theater 42
Men and Women of Letters.. 44
Architecture; About Houses and Master Carpenters....................................... 45
    Town Houses.. 49
    Country Houses 51
    Vocabulary; For Identifying the Greek Revival House.......................... 52
Map of Chillicothe 53
Points of Interest in Chillicothe... 54
This Is Ross County 59
Geology; A Story of the Time Before There Was a Scioto Valley............. 60
The Valley of the Mound Builders... 62
Shawnee and Pioneer... 66
Corn and Cattle... 70
Towns and Villages... 75
Map of Ross County.. 82
Points of Interest in the County.. 83
City and County Chronology... 87
Bibliography 88
Acknowledgments 89
Chillicothe and Ross County in Pictures... 91

GENERAL INFORMATION

Railroads: Union Depot, SE. cor. Main and Sugar Sts. Norfolk and Western R. R. (N. & W.) Baltimore and Ohio R. R. (B. & O.).

Highways: US 23, N.-S. hwy.; US 50 E.-W. hwy.; US 35, NW.-SE. hwy.; ST 104 **(To Columbus)**; ST 139 **(To Lancaster)**; ST 277 **(To Mt. Sterling)**; ST 772 **(To Summit Hill).**

Bus Lines: Union Bus Terminal, 42 E. Main St., for Valley Public Service Co., Atlantic Greyhound Lines Inc., Capitol Greyhound Lines Inc., Buckeye Stages System, Chillicothe, Jackson Coach Co., Dayton and Southeastern Lines.

Taxicabs: Three companies observe 10c rate from boundary to boundary.

Motor Vehicle Laws: Maximum speed 30 mi. per hr. No U turns at main intersections. Two hour parking limit within the business district, bounded by Walnut, Mulberry, Water, and 4th Sts.

Street Order: Houses are numbered E. to W. from Paint St. and N. to S. from Main St. Streets are numbered consecutively S. from Water St.

Accommodations: One first-class hotel, two second-class hotels. Capacity is frequently overtaxed.

Tourist Information Service: Ross County Automobile Club, 77 E. 2nd St.

Climate and Equipment: Temperate; heavy clothing necessary in winter.

Theaters: Three motion picture houses; 2 first-run, 1 second-run. Concerts in High School Auditorium.

Recreation: Softball Leagues sponsor games each evening during the summer months in Yoctangee Park, N. end Paint St. *Golf:* Chillicothe Country Club, fees $25.00 a yr., $5.50 a wk., $1.65 on Sundays, $1.10 on wk. days. *Swimming Pools:* Mead Pool, S. end of Paint St. L at Meaco Park, 25c for adults, 15c for children. Glenwood, 8 m. W. of Chillicothe on US 35 and 1 m. L. on road, 35c adm. *Riding Academies:* Black's Riding Academy, 1 m. N. of Chillicothe on US 23, E. of rd. Lessons, 1 to 1½ hrs. $2.00. Horses can be rented for $1.00 per hr. *Football:* Chillicothe High School, cor. Arch and Vine Sts. *Hunting, Fishing:* Numerous streams abounding with fish. Western section of county has supply of bird and game. Permission generally required from land owners. License required. Hunters: resident (of Ohio) $1.25; non-resident, $15.25. Anglers: resident (of Ohio) $1.10; non-resident, $3.25. Digest of state game and fishing laws issued with each license.

Liquor Regulations: On week-days, liquor for home consumption can be purchased at State Liquor Store, open Mon. to Fri. 9-10 and Saturdays 9-11:45. Consumption on premises, sold until 12 p. m. under restaurant license, 2:30 a. m. under night club license. Sale of liquor prohibited after these hours, and on Sundays, holidays, and election day.

CHILLICOTHE TODAY

Chillicothe (pop. 18,340*, alt. 643) lies in the south central section of Ohio, in the Scioto Valley surrounded by the hills of Ross County.

It is a serene and quiet town, conscious of its heritage and the tradition of earlier years when it was the most important city of a new State. For Chillicothe has deep roots and is so typical of Ohio that the hills and valley farms around it became the symbol of the State.

One morning in 1803, Thomas Worthington and his friends, who were so vitally interested in the welfare of the young State, went for an early morning walk around the Worthington estate, as the sun was rising over Mount Logan. School children are not told that they had been playing poker all night, but some people say this is the way the story goes. A more probable story states that they had been discussing affairs of state all night. These early Ohio statesmen looked across the Ohio hills as the sun rose over them and shone on the wheat fields below. They called this view the great seal of Ohio. Young William Creighton drew it and the State adopted it. Thus Ross County's image was imprinted from the beginning on the heart of the State.

Chillicothe's streets are wide and shaded; the old houses behind the trees are dignified and large, with handsome doorways. Paint Street, the main street of the town, is dominated by the stone court house with its handsome portico and tall clock tower.

The red brick business houses, built in the style of the eighties and nineties, are typical of most small towns and typical of the State. The names on these business houses, in many instances, have remained unchanged for nearly a century.

The town has followed the spirit of the times with caution. Although it is not an industrial center it has its full quota of the usual small businesses and industries. Its major industry is papermaking, started in the community as early as 1812.

Chillicothe is most important as the center of good farm country. The farmers of Ross County come to the stock auction on Wednesdays and Fridays, frequently accompanied by their wives and children who shop or go to the movies.

This is a proud city, proud of its beginnings and of its progress in the new American scene. As the first capital of Ohio it has influenced the history and development of the State. The glory and prestige of the early days are still vivid in the minds of many Chillicothe citizens who revere the traditions of their town.

Today, Chillicothe is a Saturday night town, like many Ohio towns situated in farming communities. The word Chillicothe is a part of the American language; like "Main Street" and "Babbit," it has come to have definite meaning, particularly to persons who have never been in Chillicothe. It is a funny word and has been used as a sure-fire laugh in some of the plays produced by George Tyler, a Chillicothe boy. Actually it is an approximation of an Indian term meaning "town." People in Chillicothe do not see anything funny about its sound.

*P. O. Census, 1937 — Chillicothe Population, 25,000.

THE FOUNDING OF A CITY AND A STATE

The Old State House—Hunter

Nathaniel Massie, veteran of the Revolutionary war, surveyor, speculator in furs, salt and land, came in 1793 to survey that part of the Northwest which was to become Chillicothe. He liked the Scioto Valley and planned to found a town on the land along the river which was his by right of the survey.

But the Shawnees and other Indian tribes were fighting the advance of the white man, and the white man was coming out second best in the new Ohio territory. Massie made more trips to the Scioto Valley in 1794 and 1795, but not until after the battle of Fallen Timbers under "Mad Anthony" Wayne, and the resulting peace treaty with the Indians, could settlement be contemplated with safety.

In 1796, Massie, with promises of rich lands and safety from Indian attacks, induced a number of settlers, who were only awaiting word at Massie's settlement of Manchester, in what is now Adams County, to make their way to the Scioto Valley. Twenty Scotch-Irish from Bourbon County, Kentucky, started out under the leadership of Rev. Robert W. Finley, a minister of the Presbyterian church; an equal number of Virginia Revolutionary war soldiers started from Manchester at the same time, toward land set aside in the Virginia Military District between the Scioto and the Little Miami.

Half of this group, leaving from Manchester, made its way by pirogue up the Ohio and Scioto Rivers to Paint Creek. They brought, in boats, farm implements and the heavier equipment for setting up a new community, because transportation was easier by water. The others came on horseback probably following the general course of Zane's Trace. This trace, just being laid out by Ebenezer and Jonathan Zane, was destined to pass through the town of Chillicothe in which the party later settled.

These people stopped just southeast of where Greenlawn cemetery is now and called the new village Station Prairie. The town had scarcely been started when the promoter, Nathaniel Massie, arrived to begin laying out Chillicothe. Massie offered a free "in-lot" and an "out-lot" of four acres outside the village to the first 100 settlers who could build a house during that year, 1796. The offer was tempting to the settlers at Station Prairie and it was not long before the settlement was completely deserted and its population moved into Chillicothe. Spring floods in the vicinity of Station Prairie hastened the abandonment of the town.

By 1797, Chillicothe had a population of 100, a tavern, several stores and shops, 300 acres planted in corn, and a horse mill for grinding. The town had a good start as a booming pioneer village. The population of the log cabin community was swelled by the arrival of soldiers disbanded from Wayne's army with their camp women and a boat load of Monongahela whiskey. Life in Chillicothe was pretty lively during that second year.

In 1798, more Virginians came to the Scioto Valley to establish homes; among them were the Tiffins, Worthingtons and Renicks. These young men brought with them, in addition to their education, taste and breeding, all of the material things that made luxurious and pleasant living possible. They were already wealthy men, and were not forced to take wealth from the land although they were to make agricultural history. Their coming brought a change in the character of the village. Soon it was no longer a primitive pioneer town.

Furniture, books and fine fabrics were brought from Virginia and the eastern states. Fine houses for these first families were being built. These houses, of native sandstone were modelled upon Virginia mansions, not however, lacking in their own indigenous qualities, and were adapted to the land. The British architect, Latrobe, who had been planning some of the buildings for the new Capital of the Nation at Washington, made the plans for Thomas Worthington's home, Adena. These houses were large and imposing. State dining rooms for state occasions were considered just as necessary in Chillicothe as they had been in Virginia.

Pier glass, rugs, and curtains for glass windows were brought over the mountains. Fine horses and carriages made their way down the mud streets of Chillicothe and the latest books published here and in England were sold in Chillicothe stores.

In the Northwest Territory of which Chillicothe was a part, there were 5,000 free white male inhabitants in 1798. This entitled them to a larger measure of self-government through an elected assembly. In that year the people of the Northwest Territory elected representatives to meet in Cincinnati the following year. Franchise was based on ownership of property, and the requirement set to exercise the right of vote was ownership of 50 acres of land. In order to hold office in the lower house, a man was required to have 200 acres; in the upper house, 500 acres. Thus the business of government was in the hands of the wealthier citizens of the Territory.

In this same year, Governor St. Clair cut from Adams County the rich bottom land, hills, and valleys along the Scioto and designated it a separate county named Ross in honor of a friend, James Ross, Senator from Pennsylvania. Chillicotheans wanted to name it Massie County, but were overruled by the Governor.

The first session of the Territorial Legislature was held in Cincinnati in 1799. Edward Tiffin, Samuel Findlay, Elias Langham, and Thomas Worthington were elected from Ross County. It was apparent from the beginning that this first assembly was divided into two factions. St. Clair was an ardent Federalist and in opposition to the Virginia settlers who were already looking forward to forming the State of Ohio. St. Clair used his veto often and vigorously, particularly against the formation of new counties.

The Chillicothe faction took leadership in the fight for statehood and their conception of democracy as followers of Jefferson. Actually the division seemed to fall along sectional lines. The New England and Pennsylvania settlers, principally those around Marietta, were Federalists opposing southern Democrats from Virginia and Kentucky.

The issue of making Ohio a State was a most important one, nationally. The Federalists opposed the State on general principles and because they feared that the new State's vote would give the Democrats and Jefferson the required number of votes to assume the leadership of the Nation and thereby oust their party from power.

Jefferson was elected president in 1800 and Ohio became a State in 1803 in time to help re-elect the man whose administration had granted statehood. The power of the Federalists, a strong nationalist party, was waning. It was fighting a battle to the death in the Northwest Territory.

In 1800, the Northwest Territory was divided into two parts. By ordinance, Congress established Vincennes as capital of the Indiana Territory and Chillicothe as the seat of Government for the Northwest Territory. This was a great victory for Chillicothe.

The second session of the Territorial Legislature met November 3, 1800, in Chillicothe, in the lower room of a big log house at the corner of Second and Walnut Streets. The building, owned by Basil Abrams, was known as "Abrams' Big House." There was a gambling room and bar over the assembly room on the first floor and the counter attraction at the "Big House" sometimes made the conduct of government business difficult.

The next session of the Legislature, held in Chillicothe in 1801, was very stormy. This time St. Clair and his followers were in the majority and were successful in their opposition to the new State, proposing to divide the Territory into three parts. The Governor suggested further, making the Scioto River the eastern boundary of one of the sections, thereby eliminating Chillicothe as the possible capital.

The Legislature voted to move back to Cincinnati, a triumph for St. Clair and a blow to Chillicothe. Feeling was high. On Christmas eve, in 1801, a Chillicothe mob gathered before the St. Clair home—to be held off by their townsman, Thomas Worthington, at the point of a horse pistol. The mob muttered about tar and feathers. St. Clair was persuaded, with difficulty, to make his escape by the back door.

In 1802, Thomas Worthington and Michael Baldwin went to Philadelphia, where Congress was in session, to appeal for the formation of a new State. They opposed Paul Fearing of Marietta, delegate for the Territory and friend of St. Clair, who was lobbying against the State plan. President Jefferson was, and always had been, sympathetic. It was he, who in 1784, first advocated the formation of new States from western territory. His proposals were accepted in the Ordinance of 1787. It was a precedent new to the world to accept possessions of a country as an extension of the country itself, rather than as colonies to enrich the citizens of the established nation.

Worthington and Baldwin were successful with a sympathetic Congress. In 1802, the Enabling Act was passed which allowed for a convention to set up the new State and write its first constitution.

The members of the Territorial Legislature were not to meet in Cincinnati; instead, delegates were elected to a constitutional convention which met at Chillicothe. The Territorial Legislature never met again. Edward Tiffin, Thomas Worthington, Nathaniel Massie, Michael Baldwin, and James Grubb of Chillicothe were among the 35 delegates who drew up the article of statehood.

St. Clair continued in his honest opposition to the formation of the new State, but went down to defeat. The new constitution was drawn up and the State came into existence with 34 votes for and one against. St. Clair made his last speech pleading his lost cause in Chillicothe and was soon removed from office by President Jefferson; some say for the violence of his speech.

The new State was called Ohio. Back in 1774, Jefferson had planned to give the new States fancy names like, Assenisipia, Metropotamia and Polypotamia. This was the great State of Ohio and the first materialization of Jefferson's idea, although to the everlasting gratitude of school children, such unpronounceable and unspellable names were abandoned.

In 1803, Chillicothe was established as the Capital of the State. Edward Tiffin was elected the first Governor and Thomas Worthington served as one of the first two United States Senators from Ohio. Ohio officially took its place among the other States of the union.

Delegates to the convention refused to give the new governor of the State the power of veto. The experience of the residents of the territory with St. Clair's use of the veto led them to emphasize the importance of the Legislature elected by the people.

Property qualifications for voting and holding office were not so stringent as they had been under the Territory. Free white males, over 21, who had resided in the State one year and who had paid or were charged with State or County taxes, were eligible to vote.

Chillicothe's citizens were even more prominent in State Government than they had been under the Territory. Nathaniel Massie served as the President of the Senate, Michael Baldwin as Speaker of the House, and William Creighton, a brother-in-law of Massie, as the first Secretary of State.

It was Tiffin, who, as Governor of Ohio, seized the fleet of boats being built at Marietta for Aaron Burr and accused Burr of conspiracy against the United States. Jefferson commended Tiffin for this act.

Chillicothe remained the State capital until 1810 when the seat of government was moved to Zanesville for two years. It is said that the legislators from the northern part of the State complained about the exclusive Chillicothe society and supported the change. In 1812, Chillicothe was State Capital again, serving through the War of 1812 and until 1816 when the Capital was moved to Columbus in the central section of the State.

Chillicothe furnished four governors for the State of Ohio in its early period. Three of them were young men who rode into the town on horseback in 1796. Edward Tiffin served the first and second term, from 1803 to 1807. Thomas Worthington served as the sixth governor from 1814 to 1818. Duncan McArthur served as the tenth Governor from 1830 to 1832. William Allen was the fourth Chillicothe man to serve from 1874 to 1876. He was the thirty-first Governor of the State.

Thomas Worthington

WATERWAYS AND TURNPIKES

When the spring freshets came in the Scioto Valley, awkward wooden boats called "broad horns" made their way down the Scioto to the Ohio, on to the Mississippi and down to New Orleans, loaded with grain and pork, turkeys, and miscellaneous products. Chillicothe was the Chicago of the young United States in 1800 and the years following. Later, they called Cincinnati "Porkopolis" in the language of the good farm country of Ohio.

On the outskirts of Chillicothe, men were building boats to take cargo to New Orleans. There were several boat yards; one lay at the foot of Mulberry Street, west of the present bridge over the Scioto on US 23, and the other was on Salt Creek at Londonderry. Boat building was one of the major industries in the early days. The boats were from 60 to 70 feet long, 16 feet wide and 7 feet deep. Waterways were necessary highways and the Scioto Valley had a navigable river, a tributary of the Ohio River. Other smaller streams, such as Paint Creek and Salt Creek, found their way into the Scioto and provided the territory with a kind of network of waterways, a factor inducing early settlers to make their homes in this valley.

The captains of the flatboats took their cargo on the long and dangerous trip south, in the early 1800's, and after they had disposed of it, they sold their boats for lumber and walked back home to Chillicothe. Frequently they came by boat to New York or Philadelphia and then made their way overland. There is a story of one "broad horn" that attempted to make its way up Salt Creek to Gallipolis and got lost in the hills when the water ran out.

Overland trails were few and traveling was rough and dangerous. Most of the early traces followed the buffalo and Indian trails, as did Zane's Trace, the first road to pass through Chillicothe. Zane's Trace was not completed until 1797, a year after the founding of the town. This rude pathway, begun in 1796 by Ebenezer and Jonathan Zane, started northeast of Chillicothe at what is now Wheeling, a town founded by the Zane family, and continued south to Aberdeen, Ohio, opposite Limestone, now Maysville, Kentucky.

The trace was marked by gashes on trees at the roadside with the underbrush and fallen trees cleared from its center. Zane's Trace came through Zanesville, to Lancaster in Fairfield County, entered Ross County from the northeast at Kingston and continued to Chillicothe on the east side of the Scioto. Leaving Chillicothe, the trace followed Paint Creek for about five miles and thence southwest through Pike County, into Adams County, passing through Massie's old settlement of Manchester and on to Maysville. It was the most important route of overland travel from the east for nearly four decades and very important in swelling the population of Chillicothe, facilitating trade and mail connections for the town.

In 1805, Josiah Espy came to Chillicothe over Zane's Trace. He described his journey and the town itself in his journal. Espy said,

"Chillicothe is situated on the west bank of the Scioto River, about seventy miles from its mouth, and about sixty miles from Limestone.

"It lies pretty high an a gravel bank, on a flat of great extent giving room for an immense population.

"Although heretofore (it) has been considered sickly, it has risen in wealth and population more rapidly than any in the western country.

"It is only about eight years old and it already contains nearly two hundred dwelling houses. The country on the Scioto is considered in fertility equal to any in the world, and is settling and improving rapidly. It is however, too low and flat, in consequence of which it is subject to intermitting fevers.

"These, however, are becoming less prevalent every year, and in Chillicothe for the last two years have totally disappeared; at this moment the town is perfectly healthy."

By 1803, more roads were constructed and one to Frankfort was completed. A year later the road between Chillicothe and Cincinnati was opened and from this time on the roads were gradually improved. Stage coaches were introduced, offering a far more comfortable means of travel than horseback. Even after the arrival of the railroad, the stage coach was considered by travellers much pleasanter and safer than the "newfangled contraption."

The opening of the turnpikes led to the establishment of postal connections between Chillicothe and other communities and towns. The post office was established in a rather hit or miss fashion as early as 1799. It was not until 1805, however, that a regular delivery plan was made and thirteen-year-old Andrew McIlvane was hired to carry the weekly mail between Chillicothe and Portsmouth.

The mail contract was given to two Columbus men, William and Robert Neil in 1825. The mail delivery was more regular, and a route between Chillicothe and Cincinnati was established. About 1831, when there were a dozen turnpikes in the county, agitation for free roads was begun and a daily mail route established.

In 1855, Chillicothe got two mail deliveries a day when Col. John Madeira, a resident of the town who owned the mail contract, increased his stock of horses to one hundred, making it possible to cover the mail routes much faster with the aid of fresh horses at more frequent intervals.

Today the fast train and air mail have replaced the old methods of carrying mail on horseback. Every back road in the county gets daily mail service by automobile.

The time when only the river and creeks connected one community with another and no road crossed farm land, seems remote indeed to present day residents of Ross County. Modern paved highways lead in all directions from the town, and the shallow and polluted river is deserted.

CANAL DAYS AND THE RAILROAD ERA

Along the Canal

Chillicothe was developing, and with it the entire Northwest Territory. Beyond lay a great country, its extent and potentialities only surmised, but it would be locked away forever unless transportation was provided. The trails and traces and rutted, muddy turnpikes were not sufficient for the burden that was crowding out from the east.

The Ohio Legislature in 1825 passed an act "to provide for the internal construction of canals," a step sponsored by a Chillicothe citizen, Thomas Worthington, that was to extend the frontier already thrust westward by the Erie Canal. All Ohio was excited and hopeful of a new age, and work on the Ohio-Erie Canal was started with fitting ceremony. DeWitt Clinton of New York, who had pushed the construction of the Erie Canal despite bankruptcy, corrupt politics, and mechanical difficulties, was invited to Ohio to break the first spadeful of earth. He came down from Cleveland by stage coach to Licking Summit, near Newark, and there on July 4, 1825, "while many manly men shed tears of joy," he tossed the earth into a canal wheelbarrow. Captain Ned King of Chillicothe rolled the wheelbarrow away and dumped it.

Work on the canal proceeded rapidly north and south from this point. The Akron-to-Cleveland section was opened in 1827, and by 1831 it was completed as far south as Chillicothe, giving central Ohio a waterway to Lake Erie and the East. The last section, from Chillicothe to Portsmouth, was opened in 1832, providing outlet through the Ohio and the Mississippi to the markets of the South. Chillicothe was now a port town, and produce which glutted the local market could move economically to the great trade centers. Axes, plows, and other farm implements could be brought in at a fraction of their former cost. Settlers, no longer deterred by the gruelling overland trip and encouraged by the rapidly expanding market, poured in over the new canal. Land values rose, industry came in, commerce boomed; the canal had opened a new era.

Chillicothe, therefore, had reason to rejoice, and on Saturday, October 22, 1831, when the formal opening of the canal took place, the town celebrated. In preparation for the great event, Chillicothe had erected boatyards and completed two canal boats, the *Dolphin* and the *Thomas Worthington,* the latter named for the canal's sponsor, who did not live to see its completion. At sunrise the artillery fired a salute, the Governor of Ohio, Chillicothe's Duncan McArthur, was escorted into town by the Chillicothe Independent Blues, and the celebration was on.

At ten o'clock the ladies of Chillicothe formed in front of the court house and marched to the canal, where they presented the captain of the *Dolphin* with a flag made in honor of the occasion. The two local boats then proceeded slowly up the canal to meet a flotilla of eight boats from the north, the *Chillicothe, Monticello, Victory, Canton, Lancaster, Athenian, Napoleon,* and *Citizen,* and conduct them into town to the music of the Chillicothe band. Five hundred people were on the boats and nearly 8,000 lined the banks. When the boats docked at the town, the ladies presented the captain of the *Chillicothe,* the first to arrive, with a second flag. The boats then took aboard as many as could crowd into the long, narrow cabin roofs and into the new, shining cabins, and paraded the canal for the length of the city and back to the turning basin.

After the trip, a procession formed in front of the Madeira House, and the city officials and their guests, about 300, marched to the Market House for a midday dinner at which two deer, roasted whole, were the main item of an abundant menu. The toasts and speeches lasted until 4:30. Then there were more excursions on the canal, lighted by night with torches and candles.

Four days after the celebration, the *Richmond* arrived from Cleveland with the first "all water" freight from the east for a Chillicothe firm. The next day a boat arrived with immigrants from Germany, new settlers for Chillicothe and Ross County, forerunners of a great migration along the canal to the West. The first bill of lading from Chillicothe was for one barrel of whiskey, shipped east probably as a sample of what Ohio grain could produce. During the first month of operation the canal company received $1,353.49 in freight traffic and 1,561 passengers from Chillicothe. In Cleveland, the paper and freight receipts of Chillicothe captains were being signed by a young clerk in one of the forwarding houses; his name was John D. Rockefeller.

The Ohio-Erie Canal afforded 309 miles of water way across the State with 23 locks to accommodate a fall of 88.9 feet. It got its water supply from the smaller rivers and from artificial reservoirs along the route. It was 40 feet wide at the surface, 26 at the bottom, and four feet deep. Starting at Cleveland, it paralleled the Cuyahoga River south to Akron, then followed the Tuscarawas River through New Philadelphia to Coshocton, crossed the low watershed to Newark, Hebron, and Lockbourne (where a lateral feeder extended to Columbus); then south along the Scioto Valley through Circleville and Chillicothe to Portsmouth.

The Ohio-Erie Canal was the heart of Chillicothe as well as of the State. Water Street along the canal was the busiest street in town. Wagons loaded with grain and other farm and industrial products were lined up for blocks waiting their turn for shipment. It was not only a shipping route but a passenger route as well. One good German lady, known affectionately as Aunt Kate Ringwald, came all the way from Europe to Chillicothe by water: from Germany to New York; from New York, by the Pennsylvania-Erie Canal, to Lake Erie; down from Cleveland, by the Ohio-Erie, to Chillicothe. The boat trip could also be made up the Mississippi and Ohio Rivers to Portsmouth, and up the canal to Chillicothe.

Chillicothe became an important shipping and distributing center. Throughout the Scioto Valley farmers were raising grain for shipment east and south, or for grinding at the mills that were springing up along the canal. Canal receipts for 1835 show that 86,000 barrels of flour, 96,000 bushels of wheat, and 2,500,000 staves for barrels were shipped through the canal to New York. The volume of traffic continued to increase until 1851, the peak year for the Ohio canal system.

In 1852 a fire wiped out one-fourth of Chillicothe and almost all the buildings on Water Street, the shipping headquarters of the canal. Never again did the street regain its importance, for in that same year an even greater blow befell the canal, although it was not recognized at the time. The Marietta & Cincinnati Railroad brought in its first locomotive, the *Thomas James,* named in honor of a Chillicothe citizen.

In 1825, before the canal was well under construction, Charles Carroll, last surviving signer of the Declaration of Independence, drove the first spike for the Baltimore & Ohio Railroad. In the following quarter of a century railroads pushed westward. In 1847 plans were made at Chillicothe for the Marietta & Cincinnati, based on an earlier charter. When, in 1852, the line was completed to Chillicothe, and the first locomotive steamed into town, there was no such fanfare as that which marked the opening of the canal. Railroads were still "visionary."

After 1851 the canals began to decline, slowly at first and then with disastrous rapidity. Floods and broken levees and locks interrupted the regular flow of traffic along the Ohio-Erie, and deficits mounted. At the same time, the railroads were improving in speed, safety, comfort, and miles covered. In spite of politics, deficits, and scandals, the canal managed to exist after a fashion until the flood of 1907 all but wiped out the levees and locks. Little remains but a few sections of the old canal bed to remind one of the great days when freight boats and "passenger packets" moved slowly across the State. The banks are overgrown with brush, and boys and girls fish with poles along its banks.

Chillicothe and Ross County joined with the State in making early railroad history. When Chillicothe ceased to be a canal port, much of her economic importance was gone. Still, although the county and city made no unique contribution to the rise and development of the new and revolutionary means of travel, it, like all localities, fought for the vision of increased economic development.

At the meeting in Chillicothe in 1847, Felix Renick, William H. Price, John Madeira, John L. Green, and W. Marshall Anderson of Ross County were among those chosen to serve as directors of the new railroad. The directors, in turn, elected three Ross County men to serve as officers: Felix Renick, president, William Ross, treasurer, and Seneca W. Ely, secretary.

Through this period Chillicothe was involved in the disputes and rivalries common to all communities with the vision of new empire.

The dispute over the route involved the loss of half a million dollars and in the end the railroad ran to the Queen City much the same as it does today. Hillsboro, previously on the route, was left on the end of a spur road.

The railroad boom was on. Tracks were planned on paper and stayed there; many were begun and never finished; and there were frequent mergers of the small roads with the bigger ones.

By 1860, Ross County's tracks were a part of over 30,000 miles of railroad extending over the United States. But the business of travel was difficult and dangerous. Tracks did not conform to a standard width and the difference in the gauge made it necessary to transfer from one car to another at frequent intervals. This involved tolls and additional charges. Riding was uncomfortable in the ornate painted coaches with their hard wooden seats. Wrecks were frequent, but they were looked upon as acts of God, and the railroad companies assumed no responsibility for them.

Charters were granted and money raised in the cities and towns. Through the period of boom and panic and speculation, the railroad continued to spread from the Atlantic to the Pacific, from the Lakes to the Gulf. Gradually the railroads in all parts of the country were united in great systems.

Chillicothe money was being spent and there was the vision, always, of being a railroad center with the accompanying growth and wealth.

By 1871, Chillicothe and other Ohio towns could make a direct railroad connection with the East by means of a railroad bridge over the Ohio, completed at Parkersburg by the Baltimore and Ohio Railroad Company.

The railroad reached into Cincinnati and to Marietta in 1873, over a new railroad bridge built across the Muskingum.

The Marietta and Cincinnati took up rights of way of short lines in the Hocking Valley. It was eventually bankrupt and sold, becoming the Cincinnati, Washington and Baltimore Railroad. Later the line was known as the Baltimore and Ohio Southwestern and just before the World War became a part of the Baltimore and Ohio Railroad.

Other railroads running through the county were the Dayton and Southeastern, absorbed by the B. & O. lines, and the Springfield, Jackson & Pomeroy Railroad which was later merged with the Detroit, Toledo & Ironton road, once owned by Henry Ford, and now a part of the Pennsylvania line.

In 1877, the Scioto Valley Railroad entered Chillicothe. It was to become part of the Norfolk & Western Railroad.

Today, the Baltimore and Ohio enters the county on the west, crossing Paint Creek opposite Greenfield and extends to the east for 40 miles across eight townships. The B. & O. employs around 250 trainmen in the county and from 200 to 500 men in the railroad shops in Chillicothe and in train service. It is one of the main carriers of Ross County agricultural produce.

The Norfolk & Western spans the county from north to south, crossing the B. & O. lines at the Union station. The Chesapeake & Ohio runs along the east side of the Scioto and makes one flag stop. The old Detroit, Toledo and Ironton section of the Pennsylvania line runs southeast through the county for nearly 28 miles, entering at Greenfield.

Motor traffic, developing early in the present century, demonstrated the need of hard-surface roads. In 1916 the Federal Government passed the Federal Road Act, thereby taking cognizance of the growing need. Rapid expansion of roads followed, and upon this followed a great development of truck transportation.

Chillicothe and Ross County, on three Federal highways and four State highways, has benefited materially through motorized traffic. But the earlier enthusiasm for new modes of transportation is lacking, as indeed it has been lacking throughout the country. No fanfares greet truck-trailers, no great subsidies are offered, no flags presented. Transportation has become a business; it does not have to be induced and cajoled.

INDUSTRY, PAST AND PRESENT

Chillicothe is the most important center of an agricultural community. It receives agricultural produce, grain, vegetables and beef for shipment to the larger outside markets. The town is a source of supply for farmers on the outlying districts and live stock auctions on Wednesdays and Fridays attract buyers and sellers from a large surrounding section not limited to Ross County.

In early times, the pioneer village of Chillicothe was absorbed in supplying its own needs. Food, clothing and shelter were of the first importance, consequently the earliest industries were usually the mills, operated by water power, where corn was ground and logs were sawed.

Iron nails and bricks were manufactured by hand. The pioneer, able to supply his basic needs, began to demand luxuries, and the process of their manufacture and the home demand widened the early industrial character of Chillicothe.

In 1815, the first steam flour mill was operating in the town, producing fifty barrels of flour a day. The supply was becoming greater than the demand of the home community. This led to the development of a wider trading area.

Transportation played a vital part in the rise of new industries in the town and surrounding countryside. Rude boats floated cargo down the river in the early days. In 1829 keel boats were carrying flour to New Orleans and Havana where it commanded particularly high prices. Boats returning from the South were bringing raw materials for Chillicothe's textile factories, producing woolen, cotton goods and yarn.

With the development of trade and industry, the machinery for financial transactions were set up. The first bank, the Bank of Chillicothe, built with a residence attached for the cashier, was established in 1809. A branch Bank of the United States was established in 1816 with William Creighton as president. He retained this position until 1828 when President Jackson failed to recharter the Second Bank of the United States.

In the 1830's, the Ohio-Erie Canal served as an impetus for the expansion of Chillicothe industry and particularly stimulated the production of agricultural produce. Shipment of bulky farm produce was difficult over the existing roadways, and shipment by the natural waterways was often quite expensive. Cereals now could be shipped to the East, turning toward industrial specialization, and to the South, where the staple crop of cotton was of greatest importance. Cereal mills were built along the canal. The general manufacture of small products was on the increase with the cut in shipping costs brought about by the new means of transportation.

This development was intensified with the coming of the railroad in 1852. Specialization of geographical localities became more general after the Civil War. Chillicothe's chief importance was as a marketing center for a beef raising county. In the very beginning of the town the interest of the Renicks in stock raising, breeding, and shipping indicated the possible development of the community. It is still, above all else, a beef raising community.

By 1865, Ohio was an old and established State, furnishing settlers for the far West. Through the seventies and eighties Chillicothe was a part of the industrial evolution, the expansion and development of industry that was general in the country.

By 1890 Chillicothe had two breweries, a shoe factory, a slaughter house, a furniture factory and a buggy works. Other industries located in the town were the Champion Bed Lounge factory, Valley Spokes Works, Mosher Rachet Jack factory, Chillicothe Fertilizer Works, Neely Razor Blades, Shears and Knife Factory, Scioto Grain Elevator, the A. Miller and Company Mineral Water and Pop Works, the T. Carver Fertilizer Plant and the Crown Baking Powder and Spice Works.

There were around 15,000 inhabitants in Chillicothe in 1890. Iron bridges spanned the rivers and creeks. At the Scioto Brewery they were using artificial ice to take the place of the ice cut from the canal. In 1895 the Home Telephone Company was organized and within the decade electric lights had made their appearance along with a public waterworks. In the early days of the 19th century Chillicothe manufactured the Logan automobile and established a small rubber plant. Both failed.

The major industry in Chillicothe, however, is paper making. Back in 1812, the first paper mill was established on the banks of Kinnikinnick by Hezekiah and Isaiah Ingham. Chillicothe (1938) has two paper mills, the larger, the Mead Corporation, and the second, the Chillicothe Paper Company, still largely home owned.

The Mead Corporation had its beginnings in its present location as the Entrekin, Green and Company in 1847. The plant was operated in its early days by water power furnished by Paint Creek, but in 1858 the apparatus for production of steam power was installed.

During the early period paper was made of rags and straw; after 1876 a new process involving the use of wood pulp was developed and a wood-soda pulp mill was built. The plant was purchased by the Ingham brothers and William Mills in later years.

Ingham & Mills was bought by Col. Daniel Mead of Dayton, Ohio, in 1892. The plant has been under the management of Col. Daniel Mead's son, Col. Harry Mead, and since 1905, his grandson, George H. Mead. The plant was renamed the Mead Pulp and Paper Company in 1905 and became the Mead Corporation in 1930. The Mead Corporation now has twelve affiliated units operating in eight states. It employs about 1,350 people in the Chillicothe plant and a total of some 3,500 in all plants. Daily production of all types of paper runs about 320 tons a day.

In 1919, a group of Chillicothe and Ross County residents founded the second paper mill, the Chillicothe Paper Company. This plant employs around 225 persons and manufactures writing and book paper, high grade offset bond and various types of embossed, fancy finished and color design paper.

The second plant in point of size is the United States Shoe Corporation employing 1080 people in peak production. This plant, built in 1930, is a branch of the United States Shoe Company of Cincinnati. The factory produces 4800 pair of shoes daily under the Red Cross trade mark.

The Ladoga Canning Company, successors to the Sears and Nichols Corporation, is Chilicothe's fourth industry. It provides a market for agricultural produce of the surrounding country and is a source of seasonal employment for residents of the town.

The trend of the time has been toward specialization and mass production. Chillicothe demonstrates this fact in that her industries have become less numerous but more concentrated. The majority of Chillicothe wage earners are employed in the paper mills.

CUSTOMS

MANNERS

SOCIAL LIFE

Trick Bicycle—Ireland

As the State capital, Chillicothe carried on a tradition already established with the settlement of aristocratic young Virginians, of a very gay and lively social life.

The houses themselves were built with this idea in mind, and dances and dinner parties were frequent. The ladies and gentlemen who lived in the big stone houses were charming hosts and hostesses. Their freed negro servants, knew the art of cooking and catering in the manner of the Virginian plantation. It was an exclusive society and in the opinion of the legislators from the north and west, a snobbish society.

The town itself was taking on a character quite unusual for the new state regarded by her neighbors to the east as backwoods. In 1806, Chillicothe was visited by an English gentleman, a Mr. F. Cumming, who in 1809 wrote a book with a title of bigger proportions than the book itself. It was called *"Sketches of a Tour to the Western Country, Through the States of Ohio and Kentucky. A Voyage Down the Ohio and Mississippi Rivers and a Trip Through the Mississippi Territory and a Part of West Florida. Commenced at Philadelphia in the Winter of 1809 and Concluded in 1809 by F. Cumming."*

Mr. Cumming was a gentleman of keen observation. Of Chillicothe he wrote:

"Chillicothe, which signified town in most Indian dialects, is most beautifully situated on the right bank of the Scioto, about 45 miles by land and nearly seventy following its meanders from the confluence of that river with the Ohio, between Portsmouth and Alexandria. In all that distance the river has a gentle current, and unimpeded navigation for large keels, and other craft for four feet draught of water. It continues navigable for smaller boats and batteaux upwards of 100 miles above Chillicothe towards its source to the northward from thence it glides gently through a naturally rich, level and rapidly improving country.

"The situation of the town, which is the capital of the state, is on an elevated and extensive plain of nearly ten thousand acres of as fine a soil as any in America, partly in cultivation and partly covered with its native forests.

"This farm (Fruit Hill) is nearly surrounded by the Scioto, which turning suddenly northeast from its generally southerly course, leaves the town to the southward of it and then forms a great bend to the eastward and southward.

"Water Street, which runs about east by north parallel with the Scioto, is half a mile long, and contains ninety houses. It is 84 feet wide and would be a fine street had not the river flood caved in the bank in one place near the middle, almost in the center of it. There is now a lottery on foot to raise money for securing the bank against any further encroachments of the river. Main Street parallel to Water Street is 100 feet wide, as is Market Street (now Paint) which crossed both at right angles, and in which is the market house, a neat brick building 80 feet long. The court house in the same street is neatly built of free stone, on an area of 45 by 42 feet with a semi-circular projection in the rear, in which is the bench for the judges. It has an octangular belfry rising from the roof, painted white with green lattices, which is an ornament to the town, as is the small, plain belfry of the Presbyterian meeting, a handsome brick building in Main Street; in which street also is a small brick Methodist meeting house. These are the only places of public worship in the town, if I except the court house, which is used occasionally by the Episcopalians and other sects.

"The whole number of dwelling houses in Chillicothe, as I counted them is 202, besides four brick and a few frame ones now in the building. I reckoned only six taverns with signs, which small proportion of houses of that description, speaks volumes in favor of the place. There are 14 stores, a post office and two printing offices, which each issue a gazette weekly.

"The site of the town being on gravelly soil, the streets are generally clean. The houses are of freestone, brick, or timber clap-board, the first of which is got in the neighborhood, is of whitest brown color, and excellent for building. They are mostly very good and are well painted.

"On the whole, I think Chillicothe is not exceeded in beauty of plan, situation or appearance by any other town I have seen in the western part of the United States.

"There is a remarkable Indian monument in Mr. Winship's garden in the very heart of the town. Like that at Grave Creek, it is circular at the base, about 70 or 80 feet in diameter, but differs from that by being round instead of flat on the top, which has an elevation of about 30 feet perpendicular from the level of the plain. It is formed of clay and though it has been perforated by the proprietor, nothing has been found to justify the common opinion of these mounds having been barrows or cemeteries. They talk of having it leveled, as it projects a little into Market Street, but I think it a pity to destroy any of the very few vestiges of the aboriginal population, which the country presents to the curious and inquisitive traveler.

"From a steep hill about 300 feet perpendicular height, just outside the western extremity of the town is a most charming view of the streets immediately below, under the eye like a plan on paper.

"Then the Scioto, from 100 to 150 yards wide winding on the left, and some low hills about 2 miles beyond it terminating the view to the northeast, while to the northward and southward as far as the eye can reach both ways, is spread a country, partly flat and partly rising in gentle swells, which if cultivation proceeds in equal proportion to what it has done since Chillicothe was first laid out about ten years ago, must in a very short time present one of the finest landscapes imaginable."

Mr. Cumming came to Chillicothe on foot, but was followed closely by a wagon bearing his luggage, according to an article in the *Advertiser* in 1888.

A blow was struck Chillicothe social life with the final removal of the capital to Columbus. More than one hostess must have missed the distinction of frequently entertaining visiting celebrities in connection with affairs of state.

The coming of the canal and the resultant prosperity marked the beginning of another extremely gay social era in the life of Chillicothe. The children of the wealthy Virginia settlers maintained the aristocratic ways of the town. The merchants, business men, and manufacturers who were making money on the canal built large houses and did their share of the entertaining.

There were late supper parties where fried tripe, pigs' feet and hot whiskey punch were served. The young gentlemen of the town seem to have been particularly elegant in their dress. One gentleman jokingly called the most elegant party "Mutton Swarry" according to an article printed in *The News Advertiser*. This was an exclusive party with a select invitation list. The ladies came dressed in silks, satins and velvet and the gentlemen wore black dress coats and trousers, white vest, standing collars, white cravat and white kid gloves. The black trousers were tight fitting and came down over the shoe almost to the toe. The final touch for the well dressed young man of the 1830's was a fine hemstitched linen cambric handkerchief.

Young girls, with due modesty, usually wore white muslin. The married ladies, on the other hand, wore dashing costumes of satin and velvets. The dresses were usually made with V necks, and surplice waists under which the lady wore a dainty lace chimizette. The sleeves were flowing, half length and the skirts were full. The costume was finished off with white kid gloves, and black kid slippers on white stockinged feet.

This same gentleman invented the term "Pork Swarry" for a larger and less exclusive social gathering. At a "Pork Swarry", a gentleman could wear colored pants in place of the more formal black, and could wear gloves to match his pants.

The fabrics of the wealthier people were fine. The favorite colors of the time seem to have been London brown, mulberry, olive and green. Judge Levan Belt, mayor of Chillicothe, wore a queue, knee breeches, silk stockings and low shoes with large silver buckles.

During this period of elegance and gaiety in the town, there was the panic of 1837 in the Nation. The farmers of Ross County were bringing their two-horse farm wagons into town loaded with dried apples, hard soap, beeswax, honey, apple butter, jeans, linsey, towelinen, apples, potatoes, butter, chickens and eggs, to barter for sugar, coffee, tea, dye-stuff, cotton yarn, salt and calico. The men wore homemade jeans and towelinen and the women wore calico dresses. Broadcloth sold in 1836 for $20.00 a yard.

But in the town houses, Morris O'Free, a negro caterer was arranging the parties for Chillicothe society. At the Tiffin home the silver service was identical with that used at the White House in Washington. Tiffin and President Madison had ordered silver from France.

The presidential campaign of Harrison against Van Buren in 1840 was one of the more colorful incidents in the history of the United States and of Chillicothe.

The whole country was singing:

> What has caused the great commotion—motion—motion
> Our country through?
> It is the ball that's rolling on—on—on
> For Tippecanoe and Tyler too—for Tippecanoe and Tyler too.
> And with them we'll beat little Van, Van, Van.
> Oh Van is a used up man.
> And with them we'll beat little Van.

Chillicothe folks were singing as loudly and lustily as any in the country. Log cabins with latch strings out were put up in every voting precinct in Chillicothe. The merits of the two candidates was almost the sole topic of conversation.

Harrison was the first presidential candidate to go out over the country to campaign. He came to Chillicothe by canal, wearing a buckskin hunting shirt and coonskin cap. The ladies of the town made their usual fine showing and presented him with a cane with a bullet through its handle from the battlefield of Tippecanoe.

The excitement of that campaign was never equaled by any other in Chillicothe. The stories about it are numerous and always included in any book about Chillicothe in the old days.

Chillicothe's vote helped to elect Tippecanoe and Tyler too.

Ten years after the Harrison campaign, a major social event and another famous visitor took Chillicothe by the ears. Emin Bey, emmissary of the Sultan of Turkey, arrived. He had come to this country to study educational and civic institutions. John Porter Brown, diplomat and Orientalist formerly of Chillicothe, accompanied him and brought him to visit in Chillicothe. There was vigorous competition among the various hostesses of the town, and the Turk was royally entertained. The climax of the parties came with a tremendous ball held at the old Athenaeum. Emin Bey, his secretary and attendant in their brilliant native dress, held Chillicothe society spellbound. It all ended when the emissary of the Sultan left one cold winter day by stage coach. Emin Bey, used to a warmer climate, was nearly buried underneath blankets and furs so that nothing showed but his nose and his fez. He was given a tremendous send-off by virtually the whole population and was the subject of conversation for many months after his visit. But if Chillicothe did well by Emin Bey, Emin Bey did well by Chillicotheans, and for many years after his visit, Turkish rugs, rings, mummy hands, pipes, slippers and howling dervish images were in the place of honor in a dozen or so Chillicothe homes.

After the Civil War, life in Chillicothe was affected, as life in every Ohio town was, by the new developments in manufacture and the coming of the machine age. The change was reflected in the building styles and in the forms of entertainment. The fret saw made possible remarkable complexities of decoration. Wooden curlecues, scallops, and imitation lace work began to drip from the eaves, to hang over doorways and windows.

In the seventies a new toy and means of locomotion came to delight some and terrorize the less hardy citizens. The bicycle craze had hit Chillicothe. A number of laws were passed to control the would-be speed demons, and to protect the life and limb of those who rode and those who walked.

John A. Poland, remembering the town as it was late in the seventies and early in the eighties, said:

"Chillicothe in the old days (which I think goes back to the founding of the city) considered gambling a fine art and in my time there was hardly a second story room the whole length of Paint Street from Second to Main on its east side that did not have a wide open Monte Carlo which was particularly active when we had the County Fair and Racing Season."

Poland estimated that there must have been around 30 professional gamblers in the town in these times, and 60 to 70 saloons. Even some of the groceries had small bars in the back.

Another source of entertainment for betting gentlemen was cock fighting. There were cock-fight arenas on the outskirts of the town in the various beer halls, and at one in particular, known as Smear Case Gardens.

Around this time Kirchenschlaeger's Silver Cornet Band was playing for celebrations and funerals. Hunter's String Band was also popular at the dances, where a bounding and leaping version of the waltz, and the square dance were popular.

The nineties in Chillicothe was a period unto itself with its own particular character, robust humor and sentimentality. It was an era of growing imperialism and prosperity, when people could concern themselves with manners, morals and dress. In Chillicothe, ladies were wearing the stylish leg of mutton sleeves, and bustles and it was very smart to wear a train even on a street dress. The Gibson girl was the vogue and young men sported luxuriant mustaches.

The social scene was lively with bizarre events. Great rivalry sprang up between the volunteer fire departments over which could win the race to the fire. Frequently more interest was displayed in the race than in putting out the fire. After the waterworks was built around 1881, Chillicothe got its first paid fire department. Uncle Jake Warner was the first fire chief. He always attended every fire in his own gig, usually dressed in his best suit in honor of the event.

On one occasion, a feminine admirer sent a floral piece in the form of a baseball bat to Burton Harris, a local homerun king. The floral piece was displayed publicly in one of the shop windows.

One astute business man, E. A. Herzog, owner of a Chillicothe clothing store, was the first in the city to put price marks on his sales goods and eliminate the bargaining and haggling that had been the order of the day.

There was a printer named Dan Shriner who lived in Chillicothe in the early nineties. His chief claim to fame was for his invention of the "sky foogle". The 'sky foogle", according to Shriner, was a ferocious animal that had never before been seen or captured. Shriner hired a hall, charged the eager crowd admission for a glimpse of the "terror". When the good Chillicotheans were assembled, there was a fearful rattling of chains, some horrible cries off stage and Shriner, torn and dishevelled, burst upon the scene crying, "Run for your lives, the terrible 'sky foogle' has escaped." The audience ran. They forgot to ask for their money back on the way out. Nobody ever knew what became of Shriner or, for that matter, of the "sky foogle".

The favorite gathering place for Chillicothe men, young and old, who wanted to discuss the politics of the country and the events of the world was a little side room with a sign "Tables for Ladies" off the main room in Marzluff's saloon on Paint Street. It is said that Senator Albert V. Beveridge once spent an afternoon here talking over the affairs of the Nation with the group.

It was in this room also that the Pall Bearers Association was formed. Several days before, the group had heard that a man, formerly of Chillicothe, had died in West Virginia. The man himself was not particularly popular in Chillicothe, but the group decided that never again should a Chillicothe man be buried without pall bearers to carry him to the grave. So they formed the Pall Bearers Association, a real secret society with pass words and a pin. The pin had two crossed hands with white pall bearers' gloves as a design. Later the report of the death of the former Chillicothean in West Virginia turned out to be false, but the boys kept the organization.

Lodge life played a big role in Chillicothe in the eighties and nineties and still is a very important part of the society of the town.

In the forties there had been an organization known as the "Salt Sea Crabs." In 1859 and 1860, the Sons of Malta paraded the streets at midnight carrying crosses and death's heads. According to an article in the Chillicothe *Advertiser* in 1888, "There are many who will recall the shudder that thrilled through their systems when the Grand Chief inquired in sepulchral tones, 'How many feet in the Grand Tank?' and heard the response sounding as if it came from the bottom of a well. 'Ten'. Then again rose the awful accents of the chief, 'Make it 20 and prepare the candidate for immersion'."

The Masons in Chillicothe were organized in 1805. They were followed by the Odd Fellows in 1843, and then by the Knights of Pythias, the Improved Order of Red Men, and others. Chillicotheans, as do most Americans, liked to join.

In the early 1900's, the automobile made its appearance in Chillicothe. Well protected with goggles, dusters and motor veils, Chillicothe folks set out for Sunday drives, frequently stopping to change tires. They drove Logan automobiles made in Chillicothe.

In 1907, one of the exciting events of the year was the Auto Club Tour. A cavalcade of automobiles started from Chillicothe at 9 o'clock in the morning, reached Washington Court House four hours later, went on to Mount Sterling and New Holland, and stopped in Circleville for the evening meal and was back in Chillicothe late that evening.

At the old Kite track, Barney Oldfield once raced with the Flying Dutchman and Chillicothe people watched the drivers skid around the bends where they had been used to watching the fast Chillicothe horse races.

So life went on peacefully through the early 1900's until the outbreak of war in Europe. When the United States was drawn into the conflict against Germany, the whole tempo of life changed. The building of Camp Sherman was the most hectic period of Chillicothe's hitherto rather calm and easy manner of living. After the decline and disappearance of Camp Sherman, Chillicothe was particularly affected by the post-war depression. Her social life returned to a more even keel during the 1920's and 1930's.

Chillicothe in 1938 has its clubs, lodges, churches and church organizations. The women have their literary groups, among which are the Century Club and New Century Club limited to 100 members. The men's clubs include Elks, Lions, Rotary, Eagles and Kiwanis.

Young people join, for social life and discussion groups, an organization called the Presbyweds under the auspices of the Presbyterian church, and similar church organizations.

Many of her social gatherings are held in the Elk's Hall, built as a bank in 1826, one of Chillicothe's handsome Greek Revival homes now adapted to club life, with ball-room and meeting halls. This is where Chillicothe's annual Charity Ball, the social event of the season, is held during the Christmas holidays.

Uncle Jake Warner—Ireland

CHILLICOTHE CITIZENS AND WHERE THEY CAME FROM

The Mountain House

The German people have played an important part in the growth and development of Chillicothe since its beginning. This group has been the only outside source of population, of any importance, and as such deserves special mention.

Three German hunters, Ruffner, Belans and Behrle by name, had lived and trapped in the vicinity of Chillicothe before the town was founded. These three men furnished a kind of prophecy: By 1850 half of the population was of German origin.

When Chillicothe was incorporated in 1802, two German citizens, Eberhard Herr and J. Brink, were elected to civic office.

The constitution for the State of Ohio was drafted in Chillicothe that same year; one of the members, Ogden Graff, of the constitutional convention was German.

In the new state capitol of Chillicothe, Edward Tiffin, first governor of the State, wrote the Philadelphia Immigration agent requesting German settlers for Ohio. Many of these new inhabitants came to Chillicothe as indentured servants. Their passage was paid by some resident of the town and they worked out the passage money for a period, usually three years, before establishing themselves as free citizens of the community. Between the years 1798 and 1818, approximately seventy heads of German families, tradesmen and mechanics, came to settle in Ohio, most of them in Chillicothe.

In 1817 when Thomas Worthington was in Columbus, he met a group of German immigrants who had just arrived in Ohio and were ready to choose their new home. Worthington persuaded them to come to Chillicothe.

When Emanuel Limle, millwright, Jacob Scholderer and Jacob Wolff, shoemakers, and Mr. and Mrs. Anton Pfaff arrived in Chillicothe, they walked down Paint Street to the old market house. Pausing in the middle of the street, they joined voices singing German hymns. Then they set about the business of living in a new land.

The early German settlers journeyed overland to Chillicothe, but with the building of the Ohio-Erie Canal it was possible to come all the way from the Fatherland by water. Frequent mention is made of German immigrants arriving by canal boat.

After the German uprising in 1848, German exiles came to Chillicothe. They built homes reminiscent of the Fatherland and it was about this time that Mountain House, present home of Dard Hunter, was built. They, like their countrymen who had come before them, were thrifty citizens soon involved in the social and economic life of the community.

In 1850, Chillicothe had a population of 10,000. The industries of the town, in many cases established by German settlers, included distilleries, tanneries, packing houses, cooperages, saw mills, woolen mills, a paper mill and slaughter houses.

In the north end of the city, the German settlement, common to Ohio towns, was called Goosetown. Whether the name was derived from the military goose step used in Germany or whether, because the good German housewives raised geese to supply goose liver and feathers for pillows and feather beds and thereby came the name, is a matter of conjecture.

North of Goosetown was another settlement known as Frenchtown, or Adamsville, where a small number of French settlers had made their home.

Settlers from the older states to the east who came to live in Chillicothe were frequently of Scotch-Irish or English origin.

Among the very earliest residents in the Scioto Valley and Chillicothe were freed Negro slaves from Virginia who had accompanied their former masters to the new settlement. These Negro citizens were frequently skilled workers and "Adena" was not the only large house in the neighborhood built mostly with Negro labor. Chillicothe's Negro population played an active and important part in the community.

The first attempt to give a Negro group the right to vote occurred in Chillicothe when the first constitution for the State was written. A proposal was passed to enfranchise the group of Negroes at that time residing in the State who could register their residence for one year, but later was reconsidered and failed by a few votes. A further proposal to give voting privileges to the descendants of the early Negro settlers was lost by one vote.

Although the Negro people did not gain representation under this first constitution, it was a revolutionary idea, for the time, even to consider giving the Negro the vote.

Today, there are 2,000 Negroes living in Ross County, 1800 of them in Chillicothe.

Because Chillicothe did not become an industrial center, the influx of immigrants gradually ceased during the eighties. Her foreign born population is negligible.

CHILLICOTHE AND THE WARS

Duncan McArthur

In times of pre-history, people called Mound Builders built a series of mounds north of where Chillicothe is now. Today this series of mounds is called Mound City. It is probable that Indians occupied this same territory along the banks of the Scioto. Possibly it was here that they laid out plans and mobilized their forces against the advance of the white man into Indian territory.

After the coming of the white man, the territory of Mound City was to become known as a point of mobilization in the white man's wars.

Fourteen years after the founding of Chillicothe, the United States was at war with England. The war of 1812 was foreshadowed by the stories in the *Scioto Gazette* of the impressment of American seamen by the British navy. American ships were being seized and searched, and sailors taken to serve on British ships.

On the outskirts of the town, on the west bank of the Scioto, Camp Bull was a point of mobilization. Chillicothe was the headquarters for the whole Northwest Territory.

Lieutenant Colonel McArthur of Chillicothe marched to Detroit with Chillicothe soldiers in his regiment. Later, McArthur was made a brigadier general in the northwest. Col. James Sweringen of Chillicothe marched with a small force to establish Fort Dearborn where Chicago now stands.

At home, the women were working in the fields along the Scioto because the Chillicothe men, sons of Revolutionary war soldiers, were gone to the war.

At Camp Bull, several hundred British prisoners were being held. When two British officers informed American officers of a plot to escape and blow up the stockade, four English soldiers were shot before the eyes of their fellow countrymen and co-conspirators.

A Monsieur Du Souchet opened a fencing school in Chillicothe at which he gave instructions in "military tactics and the proper training for officers." The school did not last long. Chillicothe men were getting more practical experience at the front. In all, 8,000 Scioto Valley men were in arms.

Following the American victory over the British, the country was at peace until the Mexican War, during which Chillicothe men served in the United States Army.

In 1861, the country was divided over the issue of slavery. Lincoln said, "Put down rebellion." In Chillicothe the first volunteer was John Brown, who may have been motivated by some of the same hatred of slavery as another John Brown who had come from the northern part of Ohio.

Chillicothe's men enlisted as the Chillicothe Greys. Chillicothe boys were in the famous 73rd and 63rd regiments and Chillicothe's Negro boys fought in the Fifth United States Infantry in 1863.

One of the most exciting moments of the war came when the report reached Chillicothe that John Morgan was on his way to raid the town. The militia and the home guard were summoned to be ready. Rumors and reports continued. Morgan is coming. Morgan is coming—nearer and nearer!

On Tuesday, July 14, 1864, the militia paraded and there was a mass meeting in front of the court house. The next day a guard was stationed at the old covered bridge on Paint Street to head off Morgan's cavalry so the militia could capture him. When some Chillicothe scouts, who had been out looking for Morgan, returned, the guards at the bridge were sure it was Morgan upon them. They hastily set fire to the bridge and ran like mad. It was too bad about the bridge being burned because there was less than a foot of water in Paint Creek at the time and Morgan was in Jackson, not Chillicothe.

Finally Chillicotheans got tired of waiting for Morgan, so the militia went after him. They were shot at by Morgan's men, but the shots hit the hill that protected them. Morgan never did come to Chillicothe. He was captured a little later in New Lisbon and put in the penitentiary at Columbus, from which he escaped.

Charles B. Galbreath in his History of Ohio says that Morgan was actually trying to get out of Ohio but "The squirrel hunters and the militia, however, had a way of heading him off from the river, so that he had to keep on raiding." People in Chillicothe had an exciting time while it lasted.

Lee's surrender was celebrated with great joy in Chillicothe. A few days later, her citizens, along with the rest of the country, changed gay bunting for black. Lincoln had been assassinated. Chillicothe flags were lowered to half mast and services were held in all churches.

Thirty years later, George Perkins, commander of the Chillicothe G. A. R. post, said: "We started the movement that will civilize the world and bring the happy days when war shall be no more, when the lion and the lamb shall lie down together and a little child shall lead them. Hail to a world of peace."

In 1898, Chillicothe boys were mobilized to the tune of "Hot Time in the Old Town Tonight" to fight for the liberation of Cuba. A world of peace had lasted for thirty years and in another scant seventeen years after the Spanish-American War, the whole world was to be at war again and Chillicothe was a part of that world.

When war was declared in 1917, the whole temper of living in the United States was changed. To all Americans, the war to make the world safe for democracy meant many different things. No town found its normal course of living more changed than Chillicothe, Ohio.

On the outskirts of the city, in the summer of 1917, and almost over night, a town four times the size of Chillicothe literally sprang into existence—a city of soldiers. It was called Camp Sherman and was one of the largest points of mobilization during the War.

The camp was built on a cost plus war-time basis, and finally completed at a cost of over nine million dollars, not without the usual scandal associated with the word "plus". Twenty miles of streets were built through the camp, parade grounds were leveled, plumbing installed, 2,000 frame buildings were constructed, almost over night. Labor was at a premium. Every farmer boy in the community and young men from the town got a job at the camp and wages were very high.

There were recreation halls, barracks and mess halls, and a huge Community House built in the form of a Maltese cross at the south end of the grounds as an officers club.

The camp was established for the middlewestern region of the United States, but soldiers and visitors from the four corners of the country, and the world, came to the camp before the end of the war. Soldiers from California, New York, Utah and Alabama drilled over land that had once been raised in symmetrical hills by the mound builders. The old canal lock along the edge of the camp was torn out, marking definitely the passing of the canal period.

In September, 1917, 18,000 workmen put the finishing touches to the huge military community of Camp Sherman. Between 50,000 and 75,000 recruits started pouring into Chillicothe to the camp. Mixed among the American soldiers and officers were French and English officers. Some German prisoners, some Mennonites and other conscientious objectors, were kept within the bounds of the camp. Wives, mothers and sweethearts came to stay in the town to be near their men.

Chillicothe was scared and excited. A key and lock advertisement for Ford cars in the *Scioto Gazette* warned citizens, before the camp was completed. "Be ready when the cantonment comes". Some of the town ladies probably bought extra locks for doors and windows rather than their Fords. Chillicothe was on the map as it had never been before. The town was overflowing, its population swelled to twice its normal size. Home town business men were doing a booming business. Fly-by-night vendors, fakers, tin-horn-gamblers, prostitutes and bootleggers descended on the town.

One local minister deplored the singing of songs like "I Didn't Raise My Boy To Be A Soldier" as an extreme lack of patriotism.

Some way or other Chillicothe people found room for everyone. It was every good housewife's duty to her country to take in roomers. More than one sewing room had a cot squeezed into a corner. On Mother's Day of the following Spring, there were 10,000 visitors in the town, come to see boys at the camp. Everyone of the 10,000 visitors found lodging someplace.

Ladies who had bought the extra locks were seen after church on Sunday going to their houses with two or three boys in mufti who had come for Sunday dinner. Little boys wrote in their diaries almost every Sunday, "We had a soldier for dinner". Little boy soldiers and little girl Red Cross nurses played realistically at war.

Chillicothe children were well supplied with souvenirs by friendly soldiers from the camp. Little boys had real soldiers' hats, steel helmets, gas masks, and Sam Browne belts.

The Community House was the focal point of social gaiety that had never been equaled in Chillicothe. The young ladies of the town had the time of their lives. The biggest orchestras in the country came to play for dances. Famous people and famous entertainers came to the camp both to visit and to do their patriotic duty in enlivening camp life. Paderewski, Elsie Janis, Mary Roberts Rinehart were among the visitors. Tony Sarg was a soldier in the camp. General Glen, commanding officer of the camp, was the authority in the life of every Chillicothe resident.

When the big reviews were staged, thirty and forty thousand soldiers marched on the parade ground before thousands and thousands of spectators. Nobody in the county believed the ground could ever be farmed again after it was packed by those marching feet.

Soldiers and private citizens were going to the movies and Chillicothe had her full quota of moving picture shows. Around this time, Fatty Arbuckle was being shown in "A Reckless Romeo", George M. Cohan was in "Broadway Jones" at the Star, Theda Bara, the Cincinnati siren, was playing in "Her Greatest Love" at the Royal. At the Majestic The Garden of Girls Company was playing a one-act play, "Cohan's Night Out".

In October of 1918, tragedy hit Camp Sherman—the Spanish influenza epidemic. Thousands in the camp were ill with the "flu". There were comparatively few deaths in the town but trucks filled with the bodies of soldiers drove down the streets. Caskets were piled high at Union Station. When it was all over there had been 1117 deaths at the camp.

The Armistice was the signal for the gradual destruction of Camp Sherman. After the War, wounded men were brought back to the camp for medical care. Today there is a Veterans Hospital on a section of what was once Camp Sherman.

Col. Enderlin—Ireland

The big Community House, filled to overflowing every night with soldiers, officers, visiting celebrities and townfolks of war days, burned down shortly after the Armistice. What had once been barracks and parade grounds and mess halls has gone back to farm land planted with corn and wheat. On one end of the reserve is the U. S. Reformatory. Little remains to remind Chillicotheans of Camp Sherman.

Though Chillicothe had welcomed the Armistice, the end of the camp brought depression to the over-built town. Stores and industries, that had been built to satisfy demands of the camp, disappeared. The fantastic period of camp prosperity was over and disbandment brought considerable grief to many townspeople, and the business people who had come with the camp. The depression of 1921 was one of the worst ever to hit Chillicothe and Ross County. Gradual readjustment did follow and Chillicothe resumed its position as county seat of an agricultural county.

"KNOWLEDGE BEING NECESSARY TO GOOD GOVERNMENT—"

The tradition of education for the new settlement in the Northwest Territory was provided for in the Ordinance of 1787 when the land was set aside for education and religious purposes. The Ordinance stated: "Religion, morality and knowledge being necessary to good government and the happiness of mankind, schools and the means of education shall forever be encouraged."

By 1800 a school was established at Chillicothe. It was a one-room log house built where the Royal Theater now stands and received the children whose parents could afford to pay the assessment. The tuition was based on the number of children a family had in the school and, as in most communities, teachers were probably paid rather frequently with food, clothing, and shelter instead of cash.

By 1809, the Chillicothe Academy was founded for the sons of the wealthier Virginian families. It was housed in a stone building more pretentious than the log cabin school. The boys studied, and probably complained about, Latin and Greek.

In 1820, a Mr. Steiner, an English gentleman, established a Young Ladies' Boarding School for the girls of the community who were beginning to get a little more attention. Ten years later the Female Seminary was founded by two ladies from New England, Miss Cassandra Sawyer, and Miss Eunice Strong. The two ladies were succeeded by Miss Stearns who, contrary to the usual notion of the day, thought that education should be fun. Frequently she and the old whole school quit for the afternoon to go skating.

Another school was run by Miss Mary Baskerville who wore the ruff and hair dress of Queen Elizabeth's day and looked astonishingly like England's Queen, as one account states. Miss Baskerville's school was for girls and young children and she kept discipline in a most rigid manner.

In 1826 free education was provided for by state law. In 1849 the public schools in Chillicothe were organized according to the Akron plan which provided for a grade system similar to that of the present day.

Two building sites were bought for schools in 1850 and the following year the Eastern and Western buildings were completed. In 1853, the Central building was the third school established in Chillicothe.

In 1844 the parochial school of St. Peters was organized and taught by Sisters of Notre Dame.

Chillicothe (1938) has five grade schools, a Junior High School and a Senior High School. The Mt. Logan school has a special room set aside for crippled children. The Catholic church maintains two grade schools and a junior high school.

THE PRESS

Back in 1800, Nathaniel Willis came to Chillicothe where he founded a newspaper which he called the *Scioto Gazette*. Before he came west, he had edited the *Independent Chronicle* in Boston and a paper in Virginia. Willis had been one of the "Indians" of the Boston Tea Party and according to local legend had learned the printing trade as an apprentice to Benjamin Franklin.

The early *Scioto Gazette* was a four page paper with four columns to a page, printed in large type on rough heavy paper. Under the masthead, printed in German text, was "Northwest Territory, Printed at the Seat of the Government, Chillicothe by N. Willis, Printer to the Honorable Legislature." The paper ran long communications between the editor and the representatives to the Assembly of the Northwest Territory, some news of Congress and a little news clipped from month-old Boston and Philadelphia papers.

Today the *Gazette* is one of the two evening papers in Chillicothe and the oldest paper west of the Alleghenies.

Many of the papers started in Chillicothe from time to time ended their existence by merging with the *Gazette*. Among these were the *Fredonian*, merged in 1815, the Chillicothe *Intelligencer*, merged in 1842, and the Chillicothe *Leader* in 1892. In 1892 the *Gazette* changed permanently from a weekly paper to a daily paper.

The other evening paper in Chillicothe celebrated its centennial in 1930. The *Advertiser* was founded in 1830 as the Chillicothe *Evening Post* by Wilson Cook. After a series of editors, the name of the paper was changed to the *Advertiser*. In 1900, under the ownership of George Frederick Hunter and William Hunter, the paper was merged with the *Daily News* and got its present day name, the *News Advertiser*. J. N. Hunter, son of George Hunter, is the present editor.

Chillicothe has its full quota of newspaper lore.

There is a story about Charles F. Lummis, city editor of the *Scioto Gazette*, who walked to Los Angeles, in 1884, to work on the *Times*.

Major Samuel Leffingwell, editor of the *Midland Express* around 1876 and a founder of the International Typographical Union, provided excitement for his townspeople by a unique page makeup. When he heard that the Democratic candidate, Samuel J. Tilden, had been elected, he ran a banner head, "Have You Heard the News From Maine?" and filled the rest of the page with crowing Democratic roosters. Later when Rutherford B. Hayes was awarded the election by one vote of an electoral commission, Leffingwell was hooted at by his competitors, but he calmly turned the tables by running his front page the same way but with all the little Democratic roosters turned upside down.

Billy Ireland, later cartoonist for the Columbus *Dispatch,* and a nationally known and admired artist, worked on the *Advertiser* in 1897. Ireland frequently made use of Chillicothe and Ross County material in his page "The Passing Show" in the *Dispatch*.

Others who worked on the *Advertiser* include John Bennett, novelist, H. H. Bennett, editor for many years and author of *The Flag Goes By*, and Burton Stevenson, founder of the American Library in Paris. Bennett also worked on the *Gazette*.

There are two additional papers, both of them weeklies, published within Ross County. The Clarksburg *Star* is published in Clarksburg every Friday. The paper was founded in 1926. The Kingston *Tribune*, published in Kingston every Friday, was founded in 1886.

Clough's Opera House

THE THEATER

Chillicothe has had a rich theatrical tradition that began with the usual kind of amateur performances in a frontier town and ended with the coming of the motion picture.

In 1811, the Thespian Society used to meet at William Keys' tavern for an evening of drama bordering on charades. In 1840, *Romeo and Juliet* was a local production. A great deal of fun was poked at the rising feminist movement in 1868, when Chillicothe males put on *The Spirit of '76 or The Common Woman* at the Masonic Opera House.

The real hey-day of the theater in Chillicothe, however, came in 1875 when Dr. G. W. Clough bought the old Second Presbyterian Church and made it over into Clough's Opera House. The season opened with Minnie Maddern (later Mrs. Fiske) playing "Little Eva" in *Uncle Tom's Cabin*. Not to be outdone, the Masonic Opera House was redecorated to meet the new competiton and a painter was imported from New York to decorate the ceiling. In order to pay expenses, subscription seats were sold to members. For years the seats were known by the names of their subscribers rather than by their position in the hall.

Clough had a New York manager, Col. Theodore Morris. As a result Chillicotheans had an opportunity to see the better plays and brighter stars. The townspeople went to see *The Deep Purple* with W. J. Ferguson who had been in the cast of *Our American Cousin* and was on the stage when Booth shot Abraham Lincoln. *The Stowaway, Diplomacy,* Julia Marlow in *As You Like It,* Roland Reed in *The Woman Hater,* Nat Goodwin in *Lend Me Five Shillings* all interested and thrilled Chillicothe audiences during the eighties.

Chillicotheans, stimulated by the examples before them, put on their own performances. E. S. Wenis, John Bennett, Clarence and Walter Sears, Myrtle Hill, Birdie Fisher, Puss Briggs and Annie Figlestahler were among those in the cast of *Trial By Jury*. Mrs. Lina C. Ross directed *Billee Taylor, Olivette* and *The Little Duke,* comic operas with a Chillicothe cast.

Laurence Barrett, Thomas Keane, Joe Jefferson, Lillian Russel, Fay Templeton, Pat Rooney, Buffalo Bill, George M. Cohan, Julia Marlowe, Otis Skinner, Robert Mantell, DeWolf Hopper, Conway Tearle, Kyrle Bellew, Elsie Janis, H. B. Warner, Sophie Tucker, May Robson, Patricia Collinge, Lou Tellegan and Glen Hunter all played in Chillicothe during that gay theater period of the eighties and nineties and on up through 1915.

In the eighties and nineties a young man, George C. Tyler, was making a reputation for himself. He was one of the best known theatrical producers of his time and gave the New York Theater some of its most exciting productions. George C. Tyler got his first taste of the fun of running a theater when he was manager for one season of Clough's Opera House which he renamed Clough's Grand. He was determined to give Chillicothe a big season. He did. The young star, Julia Marlowe, came to play in Chillicothe and Tyler decided to put Miss Marlowe on in *Lady of Lyons* the first night to get Chillicothe audiences used to her before she played *Twelfth Night* in boy's clothes. Tyler had a wonderful time and so did Chillicothe, but there was a big deficit. None knew it better than Tyler's father, editor of a Chillicothe paper, who had to pay most of the bills.

So George C. Tyler, the Chillicothe boy, worked himself up in the theater. He worked as advance man for plays that were being taken cross country on tour. One of his favorites was James O'Neill who played in *Monte Cristo* for 17 years. Later James O'Neill used to bring plays by his boy, Gene, to Tyler to look over. Tyler paid little attention to these early efforts of Eugene O'Neill. He was a producer in those days and was considering a man named George Bernard Shaw as a promising newcomer.

All through the Tyler era Chillicothe saw the best of the Tyler plays that went on tour. Tyler would wire his company at Pittsburgh to go on to Chillicothe. Chillicothe was a fairly small town and there may have been some grumbling in the cast, but a telegram delivered just before curtain time would clear it all up. Tyler's wire said, "This is my home town. Give it the best you've got." They did too.

Today, Chillicothe people go to Columbus or Cincinnati for most of their theater. The old Masonic Opera House has been made over into the Majestic Moving Picture Show; Clough's Grand was torn down in 1890.

There is a Little Theater group to promote the interest that most Chillicothe people have always had in the theater. *Waiting for Lefty* was presented in Chillicothe by the Little Theater group long before it was produced in some of the bigger Ohio cities. The group has put on three plays written by Charles Allen Smart and is described in his book *R. F. D.*

MEN AND WOMEN OF LETTERS

Chillicothe has a literary tradition, beginning with Martha Finley, who as "Martha Farqueharson", wrote the Elsie Dinsmore books that made at least three generations of little girls and some little boys weep bitter tears over the plight and tragedies of the saintly Elsie. Martha Finley was born in Chillicothe in 1828 and was educated in Philadelphia. She died in 1909.

Henry Holcomb Bennett, born in Chillicothe in 1863, was educated in the public schools of Chillicothe, was a student at Kenyon College, and studied landscape painting at Old Lime, Connecticut. He wrote a number of short stories, chiefly concerned with army life and is best known for his poem *The Flag Goes By*. He died in 1924.

His younger brother, John Bennett, now living in Charleston, South Carolina, was born in Chillicothe in 1865, was likewise educated in Chillicothe public schools and attended the Art Students League in New York City. His best known work is *Master Skylark*. Others of his books are *Barnaby Lee, Treasure of Peyre Gaillard, Madam Margot,* and *The Pigtail of Ah Lee Ben Loo*.

Perhaps the most widely known of all Chillicothe authors is Burton Egbert Stevenson, born in Chillicothe in 1872, author of some thirty-five novels and editor and compiler of many more volumes. He attended Princeton University and is a member of the National Institute of Arts and Letters. His best known work is *The Home Book of Verse*. Other volumes compiled and edited by Mr. Stevenson, include *Poems of American History, A Child's Guide to American Biography, Home Book of Verse for Young Folks* and *Home Book of Shakespeare Quotations*.

Among Stevenson's novels are *The Heritage, Tommy Remington's Battle, The Marathon Mystery, The Young Section Hand, Affairs of State, The Gloved Hand, Mystery of the Boule Cabinet, The Coast of Enchantment, The House Next Door* and *Villa Aurelia*.

Dard Hunter was born in Steubenville, Ohio, in 1883, and is a member of the family that for many years has owned and edited one of Chillicothe's century-old newspapers, the *News Advertiser*. He has brought Chillicothe fame as author and craftsman of books concerned with the specialized field of papermaking. Among his books are *The Art of Book Making, Primitive Paper Making, Old Papermaking in China and Japan, Papermaking Pilgrimage to Japan, Korea and China* and *Papermaking in Southern Siam*. He has compiled a number of books dealing with bibliography and methods of papermaking.

Chillicothe's most recent literary light is Charles Allen Smart, whose book *R. F. D.* concerns his personal experience as a Ross County farmer on the outskirts of Chillicothe. He is the author of two other novels, *The Brass Cannon* and *New England Holiday*.

ARCHITECTURE ABOUT HOUSES AND MASTER CARPENTERS

Adena

Chillicothe has a character and appearance all its own. It is not like Marietta and decidedly unlike towns in the northern part of the State in the old Western Reserve.

The various sections of Ohio have felt the influence of New England, Pennsylvania and the South in architecture. In the north, bordering Lake Erie, people from Connecticut, Massachusetts, and Vermont came to build their homes around the village green. Their white frame houses are dominated by the spire of the village church.

On the eastern border, the clean, red brick houses, associated with the Pennsylvania Dutch, are built even with the sidewalk.

In the Scioto Valley and southern Ohio generally, big stone houses built upon the hillside, still look down to the town in the river valley below, removed from the bustle of industry and commerce.

In the very early days, there may have been a sameness about all pioneer settlements, with their crude log cabins built for the general purpose of supplying the barest essentials of community living. After the homes were built, the pioneer turned to the construction of the log cabin church and school as next in the order of importance.

But when the pioneer stage of a settlement began to pass, the Ohio town began to assume more character of its own. The greatest difference between Ohio towns was a geographical one between northern and southern Ohio. Because the towns and villages in the Western Reserve were founded by New Englanders while those in the south were settled by Southerners, largely from Virginia and Kentucky, the vast difference in tradition and heritage was reflected in the appearance of the town itself.

Near Lake Erie, the towns centered around the church as they did in New England. Frequently the church was the most beautiful building in the town as well as the center of its religious and social life. The houses and churches were, for the most part, constructed of wood, while those in the south were much more frequently of stone and brick.

But in Chillicothe and in southern Ohio generally, the town was centered around the meeting houses where the affairs of government were carried on. Chillicothe's courthouse, which was the meeting place of the State Legislature for some twelve years, was the first public building to be built of stone in the State of Ohio.

Chillicothe was not lacking in religious principles and interests. Her traditions were different. Back on the Virginia plantations, religious services were conducted for the large households, including the slaves, on the plantation itself or at the nearest cross roads in conjunction with the neighbors of the nearest plantation. Consequently, in keeping with the tradition, the handsome churches found in northern Ohio are missing in southern Ohio.

The Worthingtons, the Renicks, the McArthurs and other Virginia settlers came to Ross County and built their homes outside the town of Chillicothe. Their farms were reproductions of the southern plantations, their homes were built in the manner of the Virginia plantation house. The style or period was generally known as Colonial and followed the Georgian or English building styles of the period with adaptations to climate and building materials.

Many of these homes still stand on the outskirts of the town. They were built of native, golden colored sandstone which was plentiful in the neighborhood. "Adena" and "Paint Hill", homes of the Worthingtons and Renicks, were completed around 1804 and 1805. They are both large houses, designed for large families and for a broad social life. There were state dining rooms and rooms large enough for parties and dancing. The kitchen at the Renick house was separate from the back of the main house, typical of the South where they had plenty of servants to take the extra steps. The kitchen and the servants' quarters at Worthington's "Adena" were in separate wings but not detached from the main house. Both "Adena" and "Paint Hill" are residences today. Another stone house of the period, completed before "Adena," was "Fruit Hill," the home of Duncan McArthur and later of William Allen. Unfortunately "Fruit Hill" burned several years ago. Descendants of the McArthurs were still living in it at the time.

Not all homes were as pretentious as these and for a long time the log cabin, the building form introduced by Swedish settlers in the Delaware Valley in 1638, continued to be the home of many Chillicothe residents. However, with the advance of the times, many of these cabins were covered with siding or were replaced by simple brick or stone houses.

Chillicothe had scarcely been founded when Jefferson started the Classical Revival in the eastern part of the United States. Monticello was the example to which more and more Americans turned when they planned imposing houses. Jefferson was designing houses for his friends and was influencing the construction of classic Roman buildings at the new capital of the Nation, Washington.

Before long Jefferson's revival of classic architecture took on a Greek Revival tinge. White pillared buildings vaguely reminiscent of the Greek temple were being built in every section of the United States.

Chillicothe was not affected by the new style until she became a port town on the Ohio-Erie canal. Then the Greek Revival building vogue hit Chillicothe in what amounted to a building boom. The new promise of prosperity brought by the canal influenced Chillicothe's merchants, business men, and manufacturers to build new Greek Revival homes.

For the most part these houses followed a general design. The main section was square with smaller additions at the back of the house. Doorways were frequently placed at one side and roofs were flat, or sometimes low pitched with smaller chimneys than in the Colonial house. The cornice was plain and frequently frieze windows at the top of the house, either round or square and sometimes covered with a wrought iron grille, served as decoration and as a means of lighting a third floor room. Bedrooms still opened on galleries at the side and back, a carry over from the Virginia Colonial house and not particularly well suited to Chillicothe's colder climate.

The beginning of this period in Chillicothe was marked by the influence of the carpenters' handbooks of Asher Benjamin of Boston and of Minard Lefever. The Adam brothers in England had already influenced the detail decoration of the Colonial house and their influence was still evident in the Greek Revival period.

There were no architects in Ross County to build these new homes but there were master carpenters, men who knew the craft of building and who followed the designs shown in the carpenters handbooks. Because these masterbuilders did not presume to original design and because their tools were simple and not adapted to the complexities of design and construction, the Greek Revival homes in Chillicothe were simple. The proportions of doorways or mantels were often strikingly beautiful. The decoration of column and doorway might be somewhat heavy handed but was still simple, direct, and with a certain vigor.

Two young architects who did a thesis on Chillicothe architecture at Ohio State University, state that the bracketed cornice ushered in the "reign of terror". As the Greek Revival building period drew to a close in 1860 and 70 it was a far cry back to the simple beauty of building when the canal was just opened.

Before the Greek Revival period ended in Chillicothe, the influence of the German Gothic made its appearance. The Mountain House, present home of Mr. Dard Hunter, is one of the finest examples of this architectural style brought to the Scioto by German refugees of the revolution of 1848. Because German people helped build the town of Chillicothe, many of the small houses are little plain brick structures with a small strip of grass in front and a beauty of their own.

In its beginning, Chillicothe was a river town. It was still a river town although the importance of the Scioto had passed. Like many towns near or in the general vicinity of the Ohio River, it was influenced by the steamboat. Houses were built which derived many of their features from the river showboat. This style is humorously known as Steamboat Gothic. The Poland House on 2nd street might be described as Steamboat Gothic, although most of the houses of this general type are frame and more ornate. It is sometimes described as Gothic Revival.

Many of Chillicothe's business buildings built in the eighties are vaguely Gothic with turrets and towers and imitation fronts and gew gaws. The library is built in what has come to be known as Collegiate Gothic, a style much used for university buildings.

Houses built in the 1920's gave Chillicothe's newer residential sections the hodge podge appearance of similar sections in most Ohio cities. More ordered and much simpler than the pretentious homes of the '90's with their bowed plate glass windows, turrets and stone carving stuck on the front, these modern homes frequently lack indigenous qualities. Imitation Queen Ann cottages, so called Colonial houses, stucco houses based on the adobe style fitted to California climate, are generally to be found. The smaller frame houses frequently fit the landscape much better.

Chillicothe too, has its poor sections. White Heaven on Western Avenue, home of three or four hundred Negroes is a slum district—not a huge tenement slum quarter but one composed of small ugly shacks and lean-tos, unpainted and frequently without window glass.

The contemporary period has seen the introduction of modern utilitarian architecture as exemplified in the buildings of several Chillicothe filling stations.

The impression of Chillicothe generally is of the Greek Revival period that dominates the main streets. In few, if any, Ohio towns can so many examples of the Greek Revival period be found. Chillicothe buildings give the town the appearance of great dignity, peace and quiet.

TOWN HOUSES

Elks' Club

Some of the more pleasing and interesting houses are listed here for the convenience of those interested in the style of Ohio houses. No attempt has been made to describe in technical terms the architectural detail of these houses other than along very general lines. For the most part they represent the Greek Revival although many are a conglomeration of several different architectural types. Frequently Greek Revival doorways have been added to Colonial houses and sometimes the doorways are more attractive than the house as a whole.

Some of the outstanding houses in Chillicothe are listed below:

POLAND HOUSE, 69 W. 2nd St.

This house might be described as Steamboat Gothic with its wealth of decoration and rather surprising detail. The white stone arches and the red brick make a very effective combination.

SMALL BUSINESS HOUSES, 64 and 68 W. 2nd St.

Both of these small, frame houses, now doctors' offices, are of typical Greek Revival style. The proportions of the fronts with their pilasters are very pleasing. Both taper back and have small side porches in the typical style of the period.

ELKS HOME, 42 W. 2nd St.

This building has been remodeled to suit its present needs and the original spacing of pillars has been destroyed. There is interesting use of iron grill railing at the side.

KING FULLERTON BROWN HOUSE, 68 E. Main St.

Edward King, local carpenter-architect, built this house in 1837. It is constructed of red brick and has a recessed upper doorway.

ST. MARY'S CONVENT, S. E. corner of 4th and Paint Sts.

This is one of the most perfectly proportioned houses in Chillicothe. It is constructed of brick, painted grey and the placement of the windows and doorways is particularly satisfying. Like the King Fullerton Brown house, it has a second story recessed doorway. An interesting grille railing crosses the second story entrance and the detail is followed in small railings at the sides of the doorway on the first floor.

REEVES WOODROW BUTLER HOUSE, S. W. corner of 4th and Paint Sts.

When Woodrow Wilson was a boy, he used to visit his Uncle Thomas Woodrow in this imposing red brick house, with handsome white wood pillars built in the Ionic Style. Interesting stone steps with a wrought iron railing lead to the entrance. The basement and first story is a little below the ground and can be reached under the front steps.

EAGLES HOME, 53 W. 4th St.

The nearest description of the architectural style of this large building, with its yellow brick walls and red tile roof would probably be California Mission. Its simpler Greek Revival neighbors furnish a startling contrast.

MCLANDBURG FULLERTON HOUSE, 68 S. Paint St.

This house is next door to the Reeves Woodrow Butler house and, like it, is built of red brick with white wood pillars. It is of excellent proportions and has a beautiful doorway.

ATWOOD WILSON HOUSE, S. W. corner of Paint and 5th Sts.

The columns of this house are of stone and quite imposing. It was built in 1845 after a design made by a Columbus architect named Kelley. The second story porch with bedrooms opening on it, on the south side, is an interesting feature showing the influence of southern architecture.

BARTLETT CUNNINGHAM HOUSE, 134 S. Paint St.

This house, built in 1850, is a particularly interesting example of the Greek Revival. It has unusual decoration over the porch and more closely resembles the Greek temple than many other products of the period.

TANGLEWOOD, Belleview Ave.

Tanglewood is one of the most beautifully situated houses within the bounds of Chillicothe. Its second story entrance, approached by stone steps with iron grille railing, lends interest to the brick house. It was used as an underground railway station before and during the Civil War. It is the home of Mrs. Walter L. Roche.

CHILDREN'S HOME, 722 Buckeye St., immediately off Western Ave.

The house has been marred by remodeling. The well proportioned porch and graceful pillars at the entrance, indicate the charm and beauty of other days. The rather crude palladian windows are interesting. The house is built of red brick and is a good example of Virginian Colonial architecture.

KENDRICK BARRETT HOUSE, Western Ave., just E. of Woodbridge Ave.

This is one of the most pleasing houses in Chillicothe. It is white painted brick with nicely proportioned square columns across the small porched main doorway and a porch running the length of a side wing. It is reminiscent of some of the smaller houses built by Jonathan Goldsmith in the northern part of the State.

THE MOUNTAIN HOUSE, Carlisle Hill, (Take Main St. road up hill, right at first St.)

Mountain House was built about 1852 by a family of refugees of the German Uprising of 1848. It's red brick walls and Gothic windows are ivy covered in the summer time. Mountain House looks down the valley to Chillicothe below—one of the best views of the town from any surrounding hilltop.

COUNTRY HOUSES

ADENA, meaning Paradise, built in the Virginia Colonial style, was begun in 1789. Thomas Worthington consulted Benjamin Henry Latrobe, British architect and surveyor of Public Buildings under Jefferson and Madison, for the design of his home.

The stone was quarried on the estate by Worthington's Negro servants and the lumber for the building was likewise from his land. Wrought iron grilles for the house were made for him by George Haynes, a mastersmith brought from the East. The glass and brass fixtures were brought in by pack train and keel boat. The wallpaper was ordered from France. Worthington lived in a two-story log house nearby and closely supervised the building of Adena. The garden was laid out in three terraces, formal beds of clipped box and dwarf iris were planted along the walks, and there were magnolia and syringa bushes.

In 1806 an English gentleman named Cuming visited Adena and described it. Cuming said, "Next morning I walked before breakfast half mile through the woods to the northward to an elegant seat belonging to Colonel Worthington. It will be finished in a few weeks and will be one of the best and most tasty homes not only in this state, but to the westward of the Allegheny mountains. It is about 60 feet square with a square roof and two large receding wings. It has two lofty stories, with six rooms on each floor and cellars and vaults beneath. The wing contains kitchen scullery, apartments for servants, etc. Like Colonel McArthur's it is built of freestone, but the stone front is all hewn and squared, like the generality of houses in the new part of Glasgow in Scotland, the stone being very similar both in color and quality. This situation is like Colonel McArthur's being on the brow of the same ridge of hills and affording nearly the same prospects. The houses were built by two Virginians of the name of Morris, who are almost self taught masons and architects and whose work and style does them much credit."

Adena is still one of the finest examples of Colonial architecture around Chillicothe. Lattice work and a bay window added to the wings, in recent years, mar the original line and mass of the building. The house is owned at the present time by George Hunter Smith and can be seen only with special permission.

PAINT HILL, built by George and Felix Renick in 1804, is of the same style and building material as Adena. More attempt has been made to keep Paint Hill as it was originally, although a small wing has been added at the side and the kitchen wing has been connected with the main house. Until recent years the block house, which served as a protection from the Indians, stood near the side of the house. Unfortunately it was torn down before the present residents bought the house. The gardens of the Paint Hill house are much like the old Virginian gardens that must have originally surrounded the house. Its walls, like Adena's, are 23 inches thick.

It is the private residence of Mr. John Traquair.

CHILLICOTHE COUNTRY CLUB. The club house has been made from what was once two separate log cabins with a roof and loft over each. There was space between the two cabins wide enough for a road. As the family grew, the space between was walled up and used. An early colonial stairway to the loft was built in this section. The original construction can still be seen inside. The mantels are handsome. This was once the old Jacobs homestead.

Other examples of early 19th Century architecture may be found in OAK HILL, the home of Mr. Charles Allen Smart, and THE CHILDRENS HOME on Western Avenue.

VOCABULARY — PRIMARILY FOR IDENTIFYING THE GREEK REVIVAL HOUSE

All of these terms are characteristic details of a Greek Revival house included here for the convenience of the reader. It should be kept in mind that the simpler forms of decoration denote the early Greek Revival, the more ornate forms denote the late Greek Revival. There are exceptions which may have depended on the taste or wealth of the owner.

Column—Composed of base, shaft and capital, a circular or square pillar which may or may not have flutes or ridges on its shaft.

Doric Column—Simplest and oldest form of Greek column with a plain capital at the top.

Ionic Column—Originally adapted from the Greek column to Roman architecture. This column has spiral volutes, derived from the ram's horn, as its capital.

Corinthian Column—Lightest and most ornate, has bell-shaped capital usually covered with acanthus leaves.

Facade—Ordinarily the front of the building but may mean the surface of any given side.

Fenestration—The term used to denote the composition of windows and doors in the wall of a building.

Frieze—Top section directly underneath the cornice.

Cornice—The projecting edge of the roof. In early Greek Revival houses the cornice was unsupported. In late Greek Revival the cornices were frequently supported by ornate brackets.

Fret—A small rectangular window usually set in the center or in a series in the frieze under the cornice at the top of the house. It frequently was covered with a fancy iron or wood grille and served both as a decoration and to admit light to an attic room.

Fanlight—Semicircular window used as decoration over a door or window.

Sidelight—Rectangular glass section used as decoration at the sides of the door.

Portico—Porch with columns across the front.

Pilasters—Treated as columns but not free standing. A kind of imitation column built in the wall.

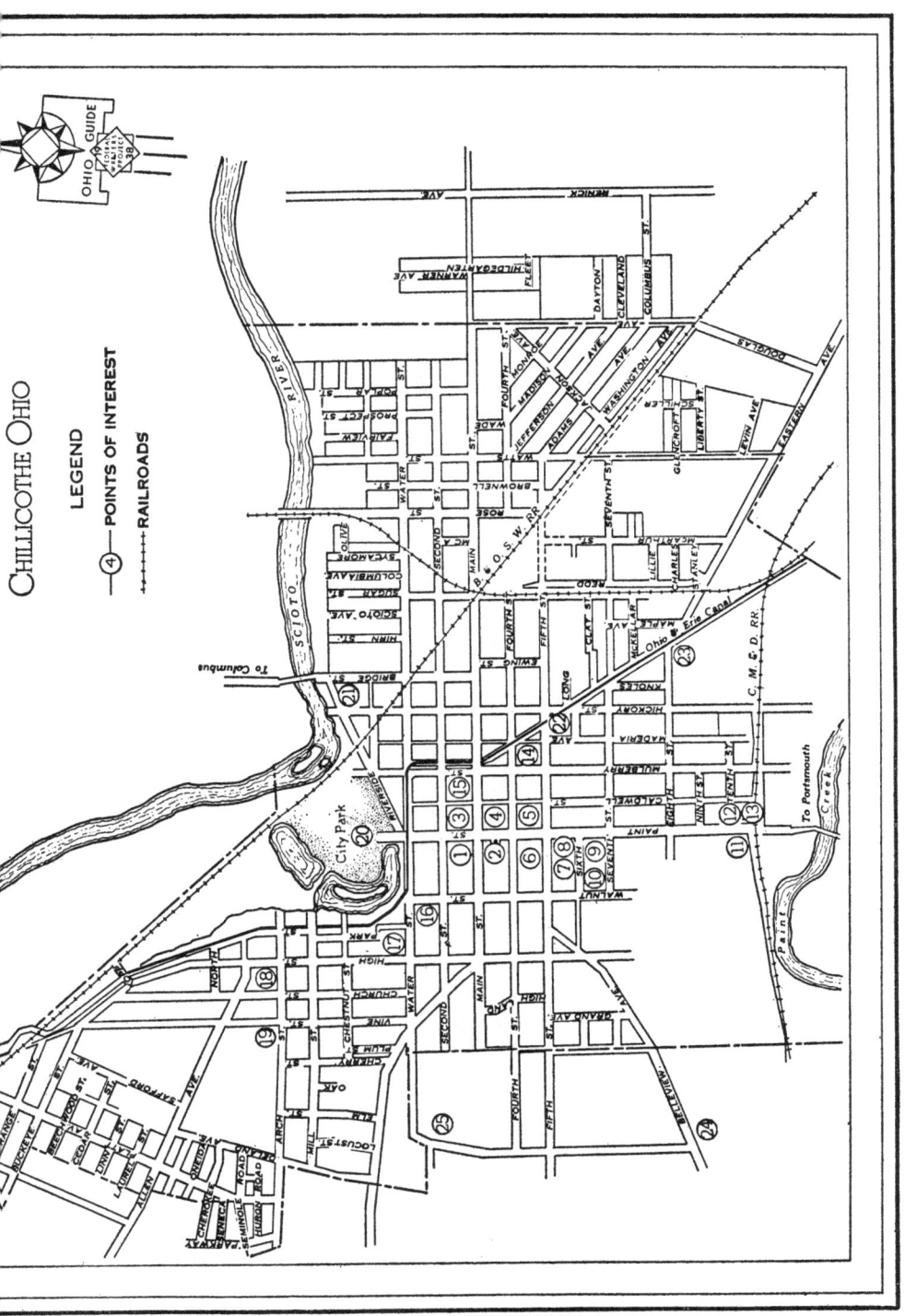

Cross Keys Tavern

POINTS OF INTEREST IN CHILLICOTHE

The places of interest in Chillicothe are listed in convenient order. The numbers are keys to positions on the accompanying map.

1. ROSS COUNTY COURT HOUSE, NW corner, Paint and Main Sts., is built of freestone in modified Greek Revival style. It occupies the site of Ohio's first State House. In 1801, before the State of Ohio was formed, the original building housed the legislature of the Northwest Territory. In 1802, the constitutional convention met here to draw up Ohio's first constitution. Chillicothe was the capital of the State until 1816 with the exception of the two-year interval from 1810 to 1812 when Zanesville was the capital. After 1816, when Columbus was designated as the state capital, Chillicothe's old stone State House, built in 1800, served again as the Ross County Court House until 1855 when it was torn down to make way for the present Court House.

The present structure was designed by Mr. E. Collins and built under the supervision of Colonel James Rowe. Many people consider it one of the handsomest court houses in the State.

2. THE CITY BUILDING, S. Paint St., between 4th and Main Sts., (W. side) built of red brick, was completed in August, 1885. The offices of the mayor, city auditor, treasurer and city engineer, and the city police station, council chambers and jail are located here.

3. THE WARNER HOTEL, N. Paint St., between 2nd and Main Sts., (E. side) was built in 1854 as the Valley House. The site has always been occupied by a tavern or hotel since the beginning of Chillicothe. Back in the days of the old Valley House, Robert McKimie, western outlaw and stage coach robber, hid from detectives in Jim Ferguson's saloon in the back of the hotel. Ferguson did not provide refuge for long but there is no record of McKimie's capture. In 1886, Jacob Warner took over the hotel and gave it the name Warner House. William McKinley, William H. Taft, Theodore Roosevelt and William Jennings Bryan have been among the guests at the Warner Hotel.

4. SITE OF THE FIRST SCHOOL, NE. cor. of Paint and 4th Sts., was first occupied by a log cabin, built in 1797 by private subscription. The first school master was an Irishman named Nathaniel Johnson. A little later a frame school was built; it had glass windows and a school bell and was quite luxurious by comparison.

5. POST OFFICE, NE. corner Paint and 5th Sts., a yellow brick building with a flight of steps leading to a columned portico, was built in 1907 and stands on the site of the old Clough's Opera House where Julia Marlowe played in "Twelfth Night" when she was a rising young theatrical star.

6. ROSS COUNTY HISTORICAL MUSEUM, *(open daily; adm. 25c)*, 45 W. 5th St., housed in a large grey painted brick residence, is conducted by the Ross County Historical Society founded January 1, 1896. On April 1, 1896, Chillicothe celebrated her first centennial and the Historical Society played a major part. When the centennial of the State of Ohio was held in 1903, the first capital was the scene of the ceremonies and the Ross County Historical Society was active in playing host to the many visitors from all parts of the State.

The Society was reorganized in 1927 and has taken on the task of collecting and saving historical data, documents and relics, relative to the history of Ross County and Chillicothe. From time to time exhibits have been arranged of shawls, coverlets and quilts, tintypes, degeurreotypes, personal photographs, group pictures pertaining to Ross County, a collection of old china, glass pewter, and other relics.

The first exhibit was held in the armory in 1927 and another at the Elk's Hall in 1933. In 1938, costumes and furniture of earlier days were exhibited in the Society's own museum. The Society was left an endowment of $20,000.00 and the building which serves as the present museum in 1933. The legacy was made in the will of Miss Petrea McClintock and Mrs. Edward W. Strong of Chillicothe in memory of their parents, William Trimble McClintock and Elizabeth Mary Atwood McClintock.

7. THE JUNIOR HIGH SCHOOL, 5th St. just W. of Paint St., was built in 1900 on the location previously occupied by the Female Seminary founded in 1830.

8. THE CHILLICOTHE PUBLIC LIBRARY, *(open week days, 9-9)* W. side of Paint St., between 5th and 6th Sts., built of stone in the Gothic style, is under the direction of Burton Stevenson. In 1893, George H. Tyler, editor of the Chillicothe Leader, told a young reporter to go out and write a story about the Chillicothe Library. His name was Burton Stevenson and since 1899 he has been its librarian. Stevenson also founded the American Library in Paris and is the author of the "Home Book of Verse" and many novels.

The building was erected in 1907 with a $30,000 Carnegie Foundation grant on a part of the old Central High School Grounds donated by the School Board.

9. WILLIAM A. (BILLY) IRELAND BIRTHPLACE, SW. cor. of 6th and Paint Sts., was the childhood home of Billy Ireland, well known cartoonist on the Columbus Dispatch for 37 years. He was best known for his page "The Passing Show" in which he frequently made mention of Chillicothe and Ross County. His first newspaper job was on a Chillicothe paper. He died in 1936 in Columbus, Ohio.

10. LUCY WEBB HAYES BIRTHPLACE, 90 W. 6th St., was the early home of the wife of President Rutherford B. Hayes. The house has since been

moved from its original location at 56 E. 4th St. to the present location. Lucy Webb met her husband at Delaware, Ohio, while attending Ohio Wesleyan University. Her family later moved to Cincinnati but she continued to visit friends in Chillicothe.

11. SULPHUR ARTESIAN WELL, W. side of S. Paint St., directly across from Mead Corporation, was sunk in a search for gas but when sulphur water was discovered instead, the search for gas stopped. At one time the water was piped into several Chillicothe houses to be used for sulphur baths which were considered to have a high medicinal value.

12. MEACO PARK *(Adm. to pool, adults, 25c; children, 15c)*, E. side of S. end of Paint St., is owned by the Mead Corporation and is operated for the benefit of their employees and the general public. It contains Chillicothe's only swimming pool in addition to a baseball diamond, tennis courts and picnic facilities.

13. THE MEAD CORPORATION, *(open to visitors by special appointment)* E. side of the S. end of Paint St., a large group of yellow brick buildings, in which paper is manufactured, is Chillicothe's biggest manufacturing plant and one of its oldest industries, with a yearly pay roll averaging over one and a half million dollars. The chemistry of paper making has been developed here to a high point for the benefit of modern production.

14. OLD INDIAN BURIAL GROUND SITE, SE. corner of 4th and Mulberry Sts., served as an early cemetery for some of the first settlers who were buried here beside the first Americans.

15. HEADQUARTERS OF GOVERNOR ARTHUR ST. CLAIR, N. side of E. Main St., 1st. residence W. of Mulberry St., was the log cabin home of the Governor of the Northwest Territory when Chillicothe served as its capitol. The logs have since been covered with siding but when the house was built in 1798, the logs were exposed and at that time there were two wings with porches running full length and a large lawn in front. Originally each room was heated by an open fireplace. The interior woodwork was all hand carved and the beams and rafters are held together with wooden pegs. It is believed that Basil Abrams, early builder and settler, built this house.

16. ABRAMS HOUSE SITE, NW. corner of 2nd and Walnut Sts., is the location of the two story log house, built in 1798 by Basil Abrams. It housed the first courts of the county and in 1800 the territorial legislature held its second session here.

The upper room of the main section was a gambling room and bar. The lower room was used by the legislature. Later on this room served for church services and a singing school. During the War of 1812, it was used as a barracks for soldiers. It was pulled down in 1840.

17. SITE OF GOVERNOR TIFFIN HOME, N. side of W. Water St., bounded by High and Park Sts., is the location of the first stone house in the region. It stood in a five acre plot and was surrounded by one of the most beautiful gardens in the Scioto Valley. Edward Tiffin was unanimously elected first Governor of the State of Ohio and continued to serve for the second term.

He came from England to Virginia in 1784 and to the Scioto Valley with his brother-in-law, Thomas Worthington, in 1798.

18. CROSS KEYS TAVERN, NW. cor. of Arch and High Sts., is believed to have been built about 1797. At that time it was a two story log house with a porch running the full length of the house both upstairs and down. The tavern was operated by one John Robinson.

It was a favorite meeting place for drovers and stock men in the early days. Later it was known for its brawls and fist fights. It ceased to be a tavern in 1860. Siding has been placed over the logs and additions have been made to the original house.

19. CHILLICOTHE HIGH SCHOOL, NW. cor. of Vine and Arch Sts., is located on the site of the old Ross County Fair Grounds. The building was completed in 1932 and on the west side of the school are the stadium and athletic field.

20. YOCTANGEE PARK, N. end of Paint St., was named in the Indian language and is an approximation of the word meaning "paint" among the Shawnee Indians who used to inhabit the Scioto Valley. The park is a part of the old bed of the Scioto River. When the railroad came to Chillicothe, the embankment of the Marietta and Cincinnati Railroad cut this territory off from the river. The land was swampy and bred fever and disease.

In 1873, the land was purchased following a special act of the state legislature providing for raising the money for the purchase from a special tax levy. The swamp was drained and in 1884 roads were built and the ground was landscaped.

The old Park Board raised money for its upkeep from the sale of ice from its lake in the winter and from rental of the grounds to carnivals and circuses in the spring.

Floods in 1898, 1907, and 1913 covered the park and caused a great deal of damage. Expense of reconstruction was great.

The cannon in front of the National Guard Armory, situated in the park, was captured from the British under Lord Dunmore at the Battle of Great Bridge, Virginia, December 9, 1775.

21. SITE OF THE FIRST PRESBYTERIAN CHURCH IN ROSS COUNTY, SW. cor. Bridge and Riverside Sts., was the scene of many of the early church services. In 1797, a young minister, William Speer, came from Chambersburgh, Pennsylvania to the year old settlement of Chillicothe. Presbyterians had been among the first settlers in Chillicothe, so young Speer was made welcome. He soon organized a church which he called New Hope Church, under the Presbytery of Transylvania. An unfinished log cabin on this site was taken over by the Presbyterians and completed as their church.

22. POLAND PARK, 5th St., between Madeira and Hickory Sts., is bordered by the old Ohio-Erie Canal on the east. The site was bought for a children's playground in 1891 and was named for one of Chillicothe's prominent citizens, William Poland. Play is supervised during the summer and the children use playground and recreational equipment provided by the city.

23. CHILLICOTHE PAPER COMPANY, SW. corner of Eastern Ave. and 8th St., consisting of a sizeable group of buildings, was organized in 1920 by citizens of Chillicothe and Ross County. It is one of the largest industrial concerns in the city.

24. GRANDVIEW CEMETERY, Belleview Hill, W. on 5th St. to Belleview Ave., L. on Belleview to entrance, is the burial place of four governors of Ohio. They are Edward Tiffin, Thomas Worthington, Duncan McArthur and William Allen.

The cemetery was first laid out in 1845 and additional land was sold by the heirs of George Renick in 1878. The graves of Nathaniel Massie, founder of Chillicothe and Billy Ireland, favorite cartoonist of this generation, are also in this cemetery.

25. MOUNTAIN HOUSE, Carlisle Hill, Main St. road to top of hill, R. at first St., is the home of Dard Hunter. Mr. Hunter is recognized as an international authority on handmade paper and is frequently said to be the only man living who has written, made the paper, cut the type, printed and published a book.

The Mountain House was built in 1848 by the Jentzens, German refugees who fled during the revolution in Germany. It is German Gothic in design and one of the interesting houses, architecturally, in the Scioto Valley. It is a private residence and not open to the public.

Edward Tiffin

THIS IS ROSS COUNTY

Ross County is a country of hills and valleys and plains, of small streams and large ones that flow into the big river, the Scioto. Its lowlands, along the rivers are rich and make good farms, but the hills are poor.

Today, the big farms and the little farms stretch over the land in every direction from Chillicothe. The small towns and villages, with their general store and usually a Methodist Episcopal church, are centered in rich land. The farmers raise corn and wheat and the county is high in beef production.

Ross County is bounded by Pickaway county on the north, Pike county on the south, Highland and Fayette counties to the west, and Vinton and Hocking counties in the east. The county covers 668 square miles and is divided into 16 townships: Paint, Paxton, Buckskin, Concord, Deerfield, Union, Twin, Scioto, Huntington, Franklin, Jefferson, Liberty, Springfield, Harrison, Green and Colerain.

The Scioto river enters the county near the middle of its northern boundary. At Chillicothe, it turns toward the southeast and leaves the county through Jefferson township on its way to the Ohio river. Paint creek, Ross County's second river in point of size, and its tributary North Fork, cut through the western part of the county to join the Scioto southeast of Chillicothe.

Upper Twin and Buckskin creeks in the west finally reach Paint Creek. Deer Creek and the Kinnikinnick in the north and Salt Creek to the south flow into the Scioto.

The wide valley of the Scioto and the rich bottoms along the smaller creeks furnish excellent farm land. At the same time there is a constant threat that floods may wipe out hundreds of acres of corn and wheat during the rainy season.

Of Ross County's total population of 45,181, the majority, some 26,000 people, make their living by raising food-stuff.

The farms range in size from 3 to more than a thousand acres, the average income per family is $520. Corn, wheat, oats, rye, barley, some tobacco and all kinds of vegetables are raised on this land. Steers and milch cows graze in the pastures and sheep on the hill side. There are vineyards and peach and apple orchards.

Farmers raise hogs and chickens and eggs, butter and milk are produced for sale in the centers of urban population nearby.

The automobile and the radio have shortened the distances, cut down the isolation of the farm house. Ross County farmers and their families go regularly into Chillicothe to see the movies and mingle with the Saturday night crowds

GEOLOGY

A STORY OF THE TIME BEFORE THERE WAS A SCIOTO VALLEY

Millions of years ago Ross County was a part of a shallow, warm salt sea, stretching between the Piedmont Plateau and the Rocky Mountains. During periods of recession, silt, sand, gravel, and calcereous ooze, the latter composed principally of the bodies of marine organisms, were deposited; these materials later were to form beds of sandstone, shale, dolomite, and limestone.

About 200 million years ago a great regional uplift occurred, the shallow sea disappeared, and its floor became the surface of the land. The flat terrain was gradually changed through the process of erosion, as rivers and streams cut their valleys, and the seasonal winds, rains, frosts, and thaws contributed their slow but ceaseless carving. Ross County's hills were formed, therefore, wholly as the result of weathering. At this ancient time the Teays, a large pre-glacial river, flowed northward, past what are now Huntington, Waverly, Chillicothe, Circleville, and St. Marys, to the Ohio-Indiana line in Mercer County.

Later, two glaciers, known as the Illinoian and the Wisconsin, crowded down from the north as far as the hills around Chillicothe, where their halt divided the topography of Ross County into two parts. The edge of the Illinoian cut diagonally across the county, northeast to southwest, from Adelphi through Chillicothe to Bainbridge.

The glacial part of the county, comprising 483 square miles, is fairly flat. This is because the progress of the great ice sheets smoothed, polished, and rounded off most of the hills, and great quantities of earth and stone—glacial debris or drift as it is known—were deposited in the valleys. Thus, the pressure and grinding of the millions of tons of ice re-created, to some extent, the condition which had existed before the process of weathering of the uplifted sea floor had fairly begun.

This activity of the ice sheets began about 300,000 years ago, and ended about 30,000 years ago. Toward the close of the age, many river valleys had been filled with debris, reversed, or diverted. Accordingly, the melt waters formed new rivers, which cut through the land, again changing its appearance, again establishing a new drainage pattern. The Scioto, with its tributary North Fork, was thus created; it flowed southward to join the Ohio, which too was formed by the melting of the ice. Ross County's Paint Creek was of similar origin.

Just as the streams and valleys tell their story of a glacial visit, so does the sub-surface offer its plain record. Borings in the glaciated section of the county frequently reveal great depths of gravel, which may be identified as of

Illinoian or Wisconsin origin. The older story—that of Ohio's great salt sea—is illustrated in this area by the frequent outcroppings of Ohio shale, a tough, black rock; Berea grit, a resistant sandstone, gray in color when exposed; and Bedford shale, a soft, gray, almost mucilaginous stratum which turns easily into clay mud.

The non-glaciated or southeastern part of the county, comprising 210 square miles, is jagged and sharp in outline in comparison with the glaciated area. In the section around Bainbridge, and along Paint Creek, impressions of small, primitive sea animals are found in the outcroppings of shale and sandstone.

Ross County's geologic past is directly related to its economic present. The quarrying of sandstone and limestone, for instance, is self-evidently important—as is the use of a soil made agriculturally productive by the deposition of a porous glacial drift.

THE VALLEY OF THE MOUND BUILDERS

The valley of the Scioto is exciting far beyond its immediate history concerning a comparatively new section of the still young United States. Perhaps nowhere in Ohio is there greater wealth of reminder of earlier inhabitants, people known as Mound Builders.

In early maps, tracing the Scioto River, made by early French explorers, there is mention of mysterious occupants of the territory called the Mesopoles, believed to have been the last remnants of the Mound Builders. Although there is no further record of them, when the first white men and women came to live in Ross county they found evidences of this earlier occupation, quite unlike any Indian culture, in the many mounds and enclosures among the hills and valleys along the Scioto and Paint creek. Since their time many of those mounds have been lost to us through the cultivation of the soil and the leveling of the earth. But in Ross County today, there are still 455 prehistoric sites composed of 370 mounds and 49 enclosures of various sizes and shapes.

Ross County is one of the most interesting sections, archaeologically in the United States and has been termed "the center of highest culture of the moundbuilding people" by William C. Mills, prominent archaeologist.

Ross County mounds fall into three different classifications, The Hopewell, The Adena, and The Fort Ancient, determined by the shape and size of the mounds themselves and by various remains taken from them during the process of excavation.

The highest culture, dating from several hundred years to 2,000 years ago according to estimate, has been given the name Hopewell after the Hopewell group found in Union township. The first mounds of this culture were examined in 1845-1846 by Squier and Davis. The Hopewell culture is said by authorities to be the most highly advanced of any north of Mexico. Mounds of this division usually occur in groups and the enclosures and mounds are more geometrically exact than most. The mounds and earthworks are shaped as circles, squares, rectangles, and crescents. It is believed that the works of this group were used for social and religious purposes rather than as means of defense. The builders of mounds classified in the Hopewell group traded with their neighbors to the north in the Great Lakes district and with those as far south as what is now North Carolina. Their pipes, particularly, show a high development of artistry and they were skilled in the art of weaving cloth. They worked in copper and silver, fashioning various kinds of ornaments. Examples of the Hopewell culture include Mound City, the Seip group, the Harness group and the High Banks works.

Next to the Hopewell group comes the Adena culture, not so advanced as the Hopewell culture but still on a high level and constructed near the same time. The builders of the mounds, falling in the Adena group, worked in copper, fashioning their own ornaments in this metal and carved stone and bone. There are very few examples of the Adena culture in Ross County. The outstanding example is the Adena mound on what used to be the Worthington estate and which gave its name as descriptive of the whole general classification of similar works. Adena mounds are recognizeable by their great size and regular shapes. The Adena Mound in Ross County was the first of this group to be examined by Squier and Davis in 1846.

The lowest and oldest cultural grouping of mounds in Ross county is called Fort Ancient, believed to range in age back 5,000 years. Most of the mounds in southern Ohio fall into this classification. The villages of the people of the Fort Ancient classification are numerous and always accompanied by burial mounds. These people used no metal; they made useful implements and weapons from flint and bone almost exclusively. There are no records of ornaments fashioned by them. The Baum and Gartner works are examples of this culture.

A better idea of the mounds and enclosures can be given through a brief description of some of them. The mounds follow, listed according to the Cultural groups into which they fall.

HOPEWELL CULTURE:

HOPEWELL GROUP, Union Township on the North Fork of Paint Creek, consist of two conjoined figures, a square, 15 acres in area, and a parallelogram, 110 acres in area. The parallelogram contains a crescent formed by seven mounds; likewise there are mounds opposite four gateways or openings in the walls of the enclosure. The circular enclosure contains one mound.

MOUND CITY, Union Township, 3 m. N. of Chillicothe on ST 104, was explored in 1846 by Mr. Ephraim George Squier and Dr. Edwin Hamilton Davis, noted archaeologists of the time and residents of Chillicothe, who gave the works their name. The enclosure and mounds of this group are among the most interesting and the objects taken from the mounds formed the most important collection found.

Over 200 pipes, pearl and stone beads, discs, copper and silver ornaments were discovered. The pipes are particularly interesting, showing a great deal of skill and high degree of artistry. The bowls of the pipes represent various animals including the panther, the bear, the wolf, the beaver, turtles, frogs, toads and rattlesnakes. In addition there are some representations of the human head. The collection is now in British museums.

The Mound City enclosure is rectangular with rounded corners and contains 23 mounds of varying sizes.

HARNESS WORKS, Liberty Township, 6 m. SE. of Chillicothe on US 23 (L) on the east bank of the Scioto, are a combination of a square and large and small circle and are located on the third bottom of the river about one mile from its present channel.

The walls of the square, approximately 4 feet in height and 1080 feet in length, are broken at the ends and in the middle by openings 30 feet wide. There are three mounds at each gateway and three mounds within the enclosure, the largest 160 feet long and 20 feet high. The enclosure covers an area of approximately 100 acres and may have been used for defensive purposes.

The large mound within the enclosure was explored in 1885 and again in 1895 by the Ohio Archeological and Historical Society. Copper plates, earrings, shell beads and some remnants of finely woven cloth were among the articles taken from the mound.

SEIP GROUP, Paxton Township, 14 m. SW. of Chillicothe on US 50 (L), is one of the largest groups within the county. The two mounds were used for burial purposes and were explored in 1908 by the Archaeological and Historical Society. The Pricer Mound is the larger and is 240 feet long and 25 feet high. The Seip Mound, about half the size of the Pricer Mound is built in three sections, the first 20 feet high, and 120 feet in diameter, the second, 12 feet high and 70 feet in diameter and the third, 6 feet high and 40 feet in diameter. The mounds are located in the center of a large circular earthwork on the third terrace of Paint Creek.

During exploration, human skeletons were found, bearing evidence of cremation as the burial method. The skeletons were found on large slabs of slate. Mica covered the floor and copper ornaments, bear teeth set with pearls, effigy eagle claws, samples of weaving, pottery and leather goods were found at the same time. The builders of these mounds carried on an extensive inter-tribal trade, as is shown by the copper from the Lake Superior region, ocean shells and alligator teeth from the south, and mica from North Carolina.

Other prehistoric works belonging to the Hopewell culture include, the Cedar Banks Works, High Banks, Dunlap Works, Blackwater Group, Junction Group, Ginther Works, Bourneville Group, Clarks Works, Hopetown Works, Turner Works and Tremper Works.

ADENA CULTURE:

ADENA MOUND, on old Worthington Estate 2 m. from Chillicothe on the west bank of the Scioto River, is one of the few mounds in Ross County belonging to the Adena culture. The mound is approximately 26 feet high and has a circumference of 445 feet. The mound was explored in 1901 by the Archaeological and Historical Society. A copper bracelet covered with cloth, a tubular pipe, flint knives, and stone tools were among the articles found.

FORT ANCIENT CULTURE:

SPRUCE HILL, Twin Township, near Bourneville, lies on the Bank of Paint Creek. It is a fortress on the high bank of the creek built in the general shape of a triangle and commands the country-side below for miles. There are traces of great fires once built within the walls of the fortress which probably were used in communicating with other tribes in the valley. The walls are crumbled and almost obliterated today.

BAUM VILLAGE, Twin Township, across Paint Creek from Bourneville, is said to be one of the most extensive and remarkable prehistoric village sites in the State. The works are situated on the first gravel terrace of Paint Creek. The site extends over a space of 18 acres that have been under cultivation since the early 1800's. Part of the works consists of a large square mound that served as a land mark to the early settlers. This is 120 feet at its base and has an area of 50 feet square on top. It is 15 feet high.

The mound was excavated in 1899, 1902 and 1903 by the Archaeological and Historical Society. Seventeen well preserved skeletons were found, and pottery, shells and bone implements.

GARTNER WORKS, Green Township, 6 m. N. of Chillicothe (E) side of Scioto, are on the site of an Indian village surrounding a large mound, 70 feet in diameter and about 7½ feet high. Traces of Indian pottery can be found on all sides of the mound.

Other mounds of Fort Ancient Culture include the Feurt and Madisonville mounds.

Nathaniel Massie

SHAWNEE AND PIONEER

Long before the white man came to Ross county, there were Shawnee villages in the Scioto Valley and before them a people later to be called Mound Builders, because they left no record of their actual name, lived here and built mounds and fortresses for the burial of their dead and the defense of their living.

White men called the Shawnees "the most conceited and warlike of the aborigines" but to other Indian tribes they were known more simply as "the salt makers." Much later the white man took over the task of salt making and we find mention of Duncan McArthur's salt well.

As early as 1693, Arnold Viele, a Dutch trader, with eleven companions camped at the mouth of the Scioto. It is probable that they may have come on up the river exchanging beads, trinkets and whiskey for Shawnee furs.

In 1739, Celeron claimed the land along the Ohio and beyond for France. Although Celeron and his party did not come to the Scioto country, it was included in New France.

About 1778, Simon Kenton, captive of the Indians, was forced to run the gantlet near the present town of Chillicothe.

After the town of Chillicothe had been established, the Reverend James Smith came across a date and some initials carved in the bark of a tree along Paint Creek. The date was 1750 and the initials T. L. and T. D. Undoubtedly, traders and missionaries had found their way into the Scioto Valley at intervals since the time of Arnold Viele. The country was full of game and the Indians had fine skins to exchange and souls to be saved.

General Harmer was in the vicinity, now Ross County, in 1790 with 1400 soldiers to fight the Indians. He suffered two severe defeats from the Shawnees and other tribes in the territory. The Indians were vigorously opposing the advance of the white man in the Ohio country although the founding of Marietta in 1788 predicted their eventual defeat.

The pioneers were opposed in these Indian wars by Cornstalk, whose town was old Chillicothe, located where Frankfort is now; by Bluejacket, who had a town of log cabins along Deer Creek; and by Tecumseh, the great Indian chief, who came from the village Picqua on the Mad River to the west.

Bluejacket's town was described by a missionary, David Jones, who visited there in 1773, as a pleasant town where he had a delicious breakfast consisting of buffalo fat, beaver's tail, hickory nuts, and boiled pumpkin.

This Bluejacket, one of the greatest Shawnee chieftains, was a white man. Today in the archives of the United States Department of War, there is a letter from one Joshua Van Sweringen of Virginia asking the Secretary of War to find his son, Marmaduke Van Sweringen, who had been captured by Indians.

Marmaduke Van Sweringen and his little brother were captured by Shawnees in 1769. The older boy made a bargain with them, offering to become one of the tribe if they would release his brother. The Indians agreed and gave him the name Bluejacket. Later Chief Bluejacket, with his adopted brothers, fought the advance of the white man, and was one of the signers of the Treaty of Greenville when peace was finally made.

After the founding of Chillicothe, when Bluejacket and other chiefs were entertained at Thomas Worthington's imposing home, Adena, Worthington's wife, Eleanor Van Sweringen Worthington, presided at the dinner party at which her first cousin, Chief Bluejacket, was guest. The relationship was probably never known to either of them.

In 1793, Nathaniel Massie, who had been through the Scioto Valley sometime earlier, determined to attempt a surveying tour along the Scioto River. In the Fall of that year, Massie set out with thirty men, among them three assistant surveyors and his chain carrier, a young man named Duncan McArthur.

The exploring party came up the Ohio River to the Scioto and on up to the mouth of Paint Creek by boat, where they set their first stake for the survey. The survey included most of Ross and Pickaway Counties and was accomplished without any disturbances from the Indians.

Two years later, Massie announced to the residents of Kentucky and his town of Manchester in Adams County his plan to found a town in the Scioto Valley.

In 1795, an exploring party set out from Manchester to select the site for settlement. When they got to Reeves Crossing on Paint Creek, they came upon a group of horses belonging to some Indians. The Indians camped nearby thought they were attempting to steal the horses and fired on them, whereupon Massie's men fired back. There was some fighting which resulted in the decision of Massie's party to return to Manchester.

The Indians, led by a chief named John, had just come from Greenville where General Anthony Wayne was negotiating his peace treaty with the Indians. For some reason or other, possibly because they got tired and didn't understand what was happening, John and his braves left while the conference was still going on. When Wayne heard of Massie's skirmish with these Indians, he scored him bitterly for creating an incident which might have destroyed the possibility of peace in the Northwest Territory.

One of Massie's companions on his various surveying trips was John McDonald, his brother-in-law. McDonald wrote an account of the Scioto

Valley as he saw it in 1796. Henry Howe later borrowed McDonald's sketches and lost them, but apparently part of his account was preserved because it is quoted in the volume of "Ohio Centennial" for 1903.

McDonald wrote, "About four or five miles above the mouth of Paint Creek, the river (Scioto) suddenly makes a bend, and runs a short distance east, thence southeast to the mouth of Paint Creek. The stream, the largest tributary of the Scioto, for four or five miles above its mouth, runs almost parallel with the Scioto. Between these two streams there is a large and beautiful bottom, four or five miles in length and varying from one to two miles in breadth and contains within the space upwards of three thousand acres. This bottom (as also the bottoms of the Scioto and Paint Creek generally) is very fertile; the loam of alluvial formation being from three to ten feet in depth. These bottoms, when first settled were generally covered by a heavy growth of timber, such as black walnut, sugar tree, buckeye, hackberry and other trees which denote a rich soil. A portion of them, however, were found destitute of timber, and formed beautiful prairies, clothed with blue grass and blue sedgegrass, which grew to the height of from 4 feet to 8 feet, and furnished a bountiful supply of pasture in summer and hay in winter, for the livestock of the settlers. The outer edges of these prairies were beautifully fringed around with the plum tree, the red and black haw, the mulberry and crab apple. In the month of May when those nurseries of nature's God were in full bloom, the sight was completely gratified, while the fragrance and delicious perfume, which filled the surrounding atmosphere, was sufficient to fill and lull the soul with ecstacies of pleasure. The western boundary of this valley, between two streams, is a hill of 200 or 300 feet in height. Its base to the south is closely washed by Paint Creek, and where this stream first enters the valley, it terminates in an abrupt point, and then extends upon the valley of the Scioto, in a northwest and north course for many miles, and forms the western boundary of the bottoms along that stream. From the point where the hill abruptly terminates at Paint Creek, running north-northeast at the distance of about one mile across the valley, you reach the bank of the Scioto, at the sudden bend it makes to the west. The valley between this bend of the Scioto and Paint Creek, immediately below the point of the hill was selected as a site for the town. This part of the valley was chosen as it consisted of the high and dry land not subject to floods of the river, which frequently inundated the valley towards the mouth of Paint Creek."

The earliest settlers in the Scioto Valley cleared land in the rich bottoms along the rivers, mentioned by McDonald, and planted corn. The first industries were the water power saw mill and the grist mill along the streams.

There were deer, elk, bear, buffalo, and wild turkeys in the woods, and at night the howl of the wolves announced their presence. In the early days the Indians sometimes acted as hunters for the wealthier farmers who settled out in the country.

Always there was a tradition of an older people attached to this land. Discovery of the many mounds, many of them now leveled and planted with corn and wheat, must have led to much speculation on the part of the first residents in this new country. The Indians, although dispossessed had left their mark upon the land. The Indian language influenced pioneer language and the first and most important settlement of Ross County was called Chillicothe, "the town," in the Shawnee tongue.

The names of the Indian chiefs were upon the lips of these people. For many years after the battle of Fallen Timbers, men spoke of Tecumseh, Logan, Bluejacket and Waw-Will-A-Way.

The white man, hungry for this western land, was to have no more serious opposition to his possession of the Scioto Valley, but still there was uncertainty, a threat, perhaps a doubt, in the mind of the settler himself as to his right to this land so long occupied by the Indian peoples.

Five years after Ross County had been created from Adams County the citizens of Chillicothe felt that there was indeed a threat of an Indian uprising. Captain Herrod, a white man living in Old Town had been killed. Nobody knew who had killed him but some people believed that the Indians were responsible. The result was that Waw-Will-A-Way, hunter for Nathaniel Massie, was killed in retaliation by some of the more hysterical and unthinking men of the community.

Tiffin, governor of the newly created State, immediately sent messengers to invite the influential Indians along the Mad and Maumee Rivers to a conference. In June, the chiefs came to Chillicothe. Bluejacket, Massas and Tecumseh of the Shawnees, Tahre, the Crane, of the Wyandots and Pahre, the Panther, of the Delaware tribe came to meet with Tiffin and Worthington and other white men of the time. The whole incident was negotiated peacefully and the Indians were entertained at dinner at Adena.

Thomas Worthington frequently had Indian guests. Mrs. Worthington had a reputation as a charming hostess. Tecumseh once split Mrs. Worthington's best drawing room curtains with his tomahawk in a fit of rage, but he remained their good friend. On one occasion Aaron Burr came calling at Adena to interest Thomas Worthington in his plan for the Louisiana Conquest. Worthington wasn't at home but Mrs. Worthington entertained Mr. Burr. Later he sent her moss roses and jessamine for her garden.

More and more settlers were coming to the Scioto Valley, attracted by the rich farm land. People continued to come from Kentucky and Virginia. Quakers from North Carolina settled in what is now Jefferson township. People from Connecticut came to take up farm land and the German settlers from Pennsylvania or directly from Europe came to start mills and to farm.

In 1804, Nathaniel Massie surveyed for the laying out of Adelphi and the following year he platted Bainbridge. During the same period the towns of Bourneville, Clarksburg, Frankfort, and Kingston were founded.

According to some of the early accounts these pioneers suffered from fever, blamed on swamp land in the bottoms. Some of the accounts go so far as to say that many people would have left the valley but that they suffered from the fever at such frequent intervals that they hadn't the strength to leave. But on the other hand, more and more people continued to come, and stayed.

CORN AND CATTLE

Deweese Farm—Ireland

The attention of the first farmers in the Scioto Valley was given to raising grain for their own consumption. Because the land was rich, the yield was great and it wasn't long before farmers were able to produce more corn than they needed. They planted young fruit bearing trees and in the course of several years the trees were bearing more fruit than the farmers could use.

There was a growing demand for food products in the eastern states, beginning to turn to manufacturing, and in the South where the planters were ignoring their food crops and devoting more and more attention to their staple crop, cotton. Still the farmers of the new West were unable to supply the growing demand because of the lack of adequate transportation facilities. Their crops of grain and fruit were far too bulky to transport over the rude roads and mountain paths to the eastern markets.

In an attempt to solve this transport problem, the settlers reduced the bulk of the grain crop by making whiskey and the fruits were made salable through their use in making brandy. Both of these products of the pioneer found a ready sale and were comparatively easy to ship over the mountains or down the rivers by boat.

Ross County residents found the Scioto was their most important roadway. Flat boats were floated down the river to New Orleans bearing pioneer products including flour, pork, beans, onions, whiskey, and brandy. Frequently keel boats, long, narrow boats that could be navigated upstream as well as down by a kind of poling and rowing process, made the trip down to New Orleans and brought back a cargo of molasses, cotton, hemp, and tobacco in exchange for their own cargo.

Land values in the eastern States were rising. The result of a scarcity of land meant that it cost more and more to raise large grain crops. As the grain furnished feed for stock there began to be a noticeable meat shortage and the price of meat was going up.

In Ross County, good farm land in the bottoms yielded as much as 100 bushels of corn per acre. It was obviously too expensive to transport this grain. In the year of 1799, there was a wagon road between Chillicothe and Portsmouth and the charge was four dollars per hundred pounds for transporting goods over that road.

Cattle needed grain for food and cattle had their own means of transport from one place to another, so Ross County farmers began raising beef cattle. As early as 1804, George Renick of Chillicothe drove the first herd of cattle over the mountains to Baltimore.

Ross County farmers began to turn their attention more and more to stock breeding. Mr. George Renick was the first to improve his breed of cattle by importing an English strain from the herd of a Mr. Patton of Kentucky.

These cattle were kept in open lots of 8 or 10 acres each. They were fed twice a day with unhusked corn and fodder and the waste was picked up by the hogs. This method, started by Ross County farmers, is still in use in some places. Ross County cattle raisers also originated the method of stacking the corn in shocks in the field which is the general practice today.

One of the most important cattle breeders was Felix Renick, brother of George Renick. In 1834, Felix Renick organized the Ohio Company for the purpose of importing thoroughbred cattle from England to improve the local strain. He went to England that same year, accompanied by two friends, and as representatives of The Ohio Company, purchased seven Shorthorn bulls and twelve Shorthorn cows which were shipped to Philadelphia and then driven overland to the Renick farm in Ross County. These were the first Shorthorn cattle to be imported into the United States.

The following year the first Shorthorn public cattle auction was held in Ross County. Some accounts state that the auction was held in Chillicothe, others state that it was held at the Renick farm, called High Rock farm, in Liberty Township.

Ross County was the most important section in the development of the cattle industry. The business of driving cattle across the mountains to the eastern markets was developing on a large scale and setting a precedent that was followed throughout Ohio and the new West.

This process of transporting cattle on foot was known as droving and the men who handled the cattle were called drovers. The drovers built up a set of social customs and traditions that are an important part of the growth of the State of Ohio and particularly of Ross County.

In 1908, the Archaeological and Historical Society of Ohio published an account of droving written by an old drover, a Reverend I. F. King, who had driven cattle and sheep across the Allegheny mountains around 1850. Mr. King's account follows: "There were two grades of cattle driven across the mountains. Three year old steers called stock cattle were taken on foot to eastern Pennsylvania, where farmers bought them and 'fed them out'. And four year old bullocks, well fatted, were also carefully driven from this state and usually sold at stock yards in the eastern cities.

"From Ohio to the eastern cities there were usually three principal routes. The northern route was by way of Dunkirk, New York State. From Dunkirk on to the eastern market, at an earlier date than that which characterized any of the other routes, the driving ceased and the shipments were made to the coast by rail and I think to some extent by canal.

"Another route was that which crossed the Ohio River by ferry at Wellsville and thence to Philadelphia by way of Pittsburgh. Soon after railroads were built west of Pittsburgh, it became a terminus for much of the stock which came in from the west, and finally this city became a great live stock market.

"The more southern route was through Zanesville, Ohio, Wheeling or Moundsville, Virginia and thence on through Bedford, Pa. to Philadelphia, or through Cumberland, Maryland, to Baltimore. It will be observed that these three routes are now substantially those of the New York Central, the Pennsylvania and the Baltimore and Ohio Railroad Lines to the east.

"During the summer and autumn, along these lines of travel, so many drovers passed that an observer, a mile or more away, could know of the passing of the stock, for far up in the air he could see long moving lines of rising dust. In the winter and early spring the clay pikes became almost impassable because of the depth of the mud. And worse than that, cattle naturally walk abreast of each other, and soldier-like they put their feet in the tracks of the one in front, and in this way great trenches were made across the highway, which when the clay dried became almost impassable for carriages and other vehicles. The condition of these roads in March and April was worse than that of the roughest corduroy bridges we have ever encountered. These 'cattle billows' were not confined to the lowlands but went over crag as well as fen. The people whose homes were located along 'the drove roads' bore patiently these discomforts, for they wished for a market for their stock and a means of selling, at home, their grain, hay and pasture.

"Along the drove roads soon were established drove stands. Some of these were inns, but more frequently, they were large farm houses where drovers obtained lodging and board as well as provisions for the stock they were transporting. During the thirty years, beginning with 1822, when droving began it was a common thing for corn to sell for twenty-five cents a bushel or for thirty seven and a half cents per shock. In that period cattle usually could be bought in the autumn for two or three cents a pound, gross weight and hogs only a little above these figures. A good fat sheep could be bought for one dollar and a quarter, and choice ones at two dollars.

"The owner or conductor of the drove was known as "the boss". These men even on their second trip across the mountains became familiar with all the drove stands. And in their minds these were all graded. No man along the southern route had such a good reputation as Mr. Ezekial Bundy, whose farmhouse stood a few miles east of Barnesville, Ohio. He set the best table and furnished the best beds to sleep in, of any of them, and his bills were not higher than those whose accommodations were much inferior. Mr. Rex, whose home was near Jefferson, Pa., was a favorite place to stop over the Sabbath.

"Seldom was there less than one hundred cattle in a drove, and not often much over two hundred in the largest droves. When fat cattle were driven, it was not unusual to have the drove accompanied with as many or even more stock hogs. In such cases the hogs cost little in the way of grain, for they consumed the corn that the cattle wasted. When the hogs were taken with the cattle the journey took about a week longer. Droves of horses would average 22 miles a day, stock cattle nine miles, fat cattle seven, and cattle with hogs not quite so many miles per day. The crew to take care of a drove of cattle consisted of a boss who rode on horseback seated on a pair of saddlebags which contained a change of linen for himself and the men who were afoot. On his saddle pad was a roll of extra garments, for use by the crew in stormy weather. Of course he was armed with a good blacksnake whip. In large droves, a second man was also mounted in the same manner as the boss. He too, had in his hand a Centerville whip. A harnessmaker in a little Ohio village called Centerville, in Belmont County, was known to all southern route drivers to make the best whips and sell them at reasonable prices. These whips had linen or silken crackers and when used by a man who knew how, would make a report like the firing of a rifle. This extra man on horseback was needed to keep the stock in place when passing through forests and when the drove passed intersecting roads and streets. With cattle there was a man on foot leading an ox by a rope attached to his horns. For the reader will please note, that the art of dehorning was not then in vogue. Not one steer in fifty was a mulley. Soon after going on the road the other bullocks learned to follow the lead ox.

"In the rear of the drove, another man, usually afoot, armed also with a whip, which was well used on belated and lazy steers.

"At the luncheon hour the whole drove was halted in some well shaded lot, where perhaps every bullock rested by lying down and happy was the crew that by any means could supply itself with a luncheon. While the cattle were thus resting, it was the custom for the boss to ride rapidly ahead and make arrangements for pasture and food for man and beast during the night.

"Drove hands in these days received fifteen dollars per month. And having reached the market they usually walked home again. It was a rule to allow 33 miles as a day's task. Some swift walkers were able to make an average of 40 miles per day. And in this way, in five days he made an extra half dollar plus another fifty cent piece which he was allowed for a days meals and lodging. These men traversed the same road that was used in going east, so as to settle for stock left accidentally in the field, or that was left because it became lame or sick. The men who kept drove stands could be relied upon to care well for such stock and in the end to pay a fair price for such as were accidentally left.

"It often occurred that in passing over macadamized roads, and indeed over other roads which were rocky, that the bullocks feet became tender, and soon the animal became lame, and shoeing was necessary. Along such highways were located blacksmiths who had stalls and machinery to lift the steer off his feet so he could be shod and thus prepare to finish the journey.

"At that period bridge tolls and ferry fees were high. For this reason, and because in many cases there were no bridges, it was not unusual in crossing large rivers to put the lead ox and some ten more bullocks on a ferry boat, and these became the leaders, and the balance of the drove by a little coercing were made to follow by swimimng the river.

"In the seasons of the year when it was necessary to feed corn it was the custom to use that which was in the shock, throw it on a wagon, and go to the feed lot and while the wagon was moving toss off the corn until the wagon was empty. When the corn was in the ear, men with scoop shovels threw off while the wagon was moving. This required no little skill and trained muscle.

"We have already stated that the price paid the stock raiser was low, but the drover did not always make money, for it took some forty or fifty days to reach the market, and in that time there might be great fluctuations. To wait in the East for a better market was to be at no little expense, for grain and pasture then in the East was much higher in price than in Ohio.

"It was not uncommon for the drover to be met by speculators some three or four days journey from the market. These were men who were good judges of stock and they knew well how the market was supplied and how prices ruled. To a great extent they had the advantage of the drover, who did not have access to a daily market report, only as he might interview returning drovers.

"These speculators made money more rapidly and surely than the drover. At the same time the Ohio drover usually made money. Often his profit was a handsome sum, and the result of other trips was a great loss."

Mr. King says further—"The transporting of cattle, horses, sheep and hogs, (indeed in some cases, turkeys) in droves from Ohio and quite a number of other states, even as far west as Missouri, continued until the lines of railroads were ready for use, connecting with the eastern cities.

"In the settlement of Ohio there was such an abundance of timber that fences were inexpensive and we had in the state so little prairie, that in stock raising, we did not need herdsmen as was needed in the following years in states farther west, so neither the Ohio drover nor his employee was ever known by the term "cowboy".

A Mr. Daniel Drew was the tavernkeeper at the Bull's Head Tavern in New York city where the Ross County drovers stopped. The tavern had a stock yards in connection and the cattle as well as the men could be put up. Droving was very profitable to Mr. Drew for when he died he endowed the Drew Theological Seminary, in Madison, New Jersey.

The coming of the canal made possible regular transport of grain to the East and South. The railroad was a more speedy and direct method of transporting beef cattle and with the coming of refrigeration, the stockyard industry passed to the West and centered in Chicago. Today, Ross County still raises beef cattle, and ranks among the leading counties of the State in beef production.

Ross County farmers and their families belong to the Grange, buy supplies and market their produce through the Ohio Farm Bureau.

The first County Fair in the State was held in Chillicothe in 1833, and since that time, farmers and their wives have participated in raising agricultural standards and examination of new methods and machinery through the agricultural Fair. Today Ross County farmers participate in the State Fair held annually in Columbus.

TOWNS AND VILLAGES

ADELPHI—(alt. 800, pop. 412) *18 m.* NE. of Chillicothe on ST 180 and ST 56.

Nathaniel Massie surveyed the site of Adelphi for Basil and Reubin Abrams and the town was platted in 1804. It was named by Massie after Adelphia in Pennsylvania and was incorporated in 1838.

The town lies on a level plateau in the midst of farming country between the Salt Creek valley to the northeast and the uplands of the west and south. Brimstone Creek flows near the southern border of the town and empties into Salt Creek. The town is in a mineral well region and at one time Mineral Spring Ground in the north of the town was a health resort. Adelphi wells have iron, sulphur, and lime traces.

German Lutherans laid out a cemetery here before the town was platted. It is said to be one of the oldest cemeteries in the State and lies north of the town.

Adelphi has a few small industries, a bank, post office, a Methodist Episcopal church, an elementary and a high school.

ALMA—(alt. 820, pop. 75) *11.2 m.* S. of Chillicothe on US 23.

Early settlers came to this location in the highlands to avoid the ague prevalent in the low lands. They called it Pleasant Valley, but when the post office was established in 1868 the name was changed to Alma. Among the settlers who came in 1850 were the Wiltshire and Cooper families.

About Civil War times, the town was best known for its many cooper shops.

Today Alma has a two room school and a Methodist Episcopal church. Crooked Creek runs along one side and to the northeast is a State forest preserve of 3,300 acres.

ANDERSONVILLE—(alt. 845, pop. 75) *6 m.* N. of Chillicothe on ST 104.

Mahlon Anderson, owner of this land, platted the town and called it Andersonville around 1845. In 1850 he sold the land to Major and Lorenzo Dunlap, who had Colonel Lewis Sifferd survey it, and renamed the town Lewisville. When the post office was established in 1873 the town was called Andersonville again. There is one church, the Methodist Episcopal. Atlantic Greyhound busses pass through the town.

AUSTIN—(alt. 764, pop. 35) *3 m.* W. of Frankfort on US 35.

Austin Bush built a flour mill here on the North Fork of Paint Creek in 1836. The post office was established in 1849 and given the name of Austin in his honor. There is one Methodist Episcopal church.

BAINBRIDGE—(alt. 716, pop. 800) *20 m.* SW. of Chillicothe on US 50.

The first settlement in this locality was called New Amsterdam and was located up Paint Creek about two miles from the present town. New Amsterdam was founded in 1800 by the Smith brothers, who built a saw mill along the creek.

In 1805, the settlers of New Amsterdam moved to the present site of Bainbridge because the swampy land at the old site subjected them to fevers.

Nathaniel Massie surveyed the site and named it after a close friend, Commodore Bainbridge.

At one time, Bainbridge had aspirations to become a county seat. Its citizens promoted a plan to form another county from Ross County to be called Massie county. The people of Bainbridge were so sure of success that they built the Massie County Courthouse in the county that was never created. The courthouse still stands in Bainbridge and is being used as an apartment house.

In 1826, Dr. John Harris started a school for dentists here, and consequently Bainbridge today lays claim to being the birthplace of modern dentistry. Chapin Harris, his brother and student, was the editor of the first *American Journal of Dental Science* in 1839 and founder of the first dental college in Baltimore in 1840. Others of Dr. Chapin's students at the little school in Bainbridge, include James Taylor, founder of the Ohio College of Dental Science at Cincinnati in 1845-47, John Allen who invented continuous gum work, Edward P. Church who invented forceps for extracting upper third molars and Wesley Sampler who pulled the first tooth Abraham Lincoln had extracted.

The village was incorporated in 1838. Today it has a public library and three churches, Methodist Episcopal, Presbyterian, and African Methodist Episcopal. There is a flour mill, producing 75 barrels a day, and a bank serving the surrounding community. Motion pictures are shown in the township hall.

One of Bainbridge's famous citizens is Clyde Beatty, wild animal trainer and owner of a circus company.

BIERS RUN—(alt. 796, pop. 10) 9 *m.* NW. of Chillicothe on US 35.

The few houses of this little settlement are along the creek from which the community got its name.

BOURNEVILLE—(alt. 681, pop. 200) 9 *m.* SW. of Chillicothe on US 50.

Settlers came to this land in Paint Creek Valley as early as 1796, the same year that Chillicothe was founded. Two years later the first wedding to be celebrated in the Scioto Valley was held in this settlement when Elizabeth Cochran, who had come with her father Hugh Cochran from Lexington, Kentucky, married George Kilgore. The young pioneer couple were married by a circuit riding preacher who happened to be in the neighborhood. The village of Bourneville was not platted until 1832 by Isaac McCrackin and John Boswell who named it in honor of the surveyor, Colonel Bourne.

Bourneville is a small, one-street town situated in a farming community. Its small frame and brick houses are set close to the street.

The Capitol Greyhound Bus Lines pass through it from Chillicothe to Cincinnati.

CLARKSBURG—(alt. 771, pop. 450) *16 m.* NW. of Chillicothe on ST 277.

Pioneers arrived in this locality around 1800. In 1815, a saw mill and grist mill were built, helping the settlers already there and attracting new ones. The town was named after Colonel William Clark, a veteran of the war of 1812 and an early settler, credited with the real founding of the town.

The town has two churches, the Christian and the Methodist Episcopal, a town hall, a grade school and high school and the First Commercial Bank.

DENVER—(alt. 836, pop. 100) *11 m.* S. of Chillicothe on the Waverly-Denver road.

Founded on the banks of Crooked Creek around 1850, the settlement was first called Farmersville. It was more commonly known as "Hoop-Pole" because of the number of cooper shops making barrels there. When the post office was established the name was changed to Denver after Denver, Colorado.

FRANKFORT—(alt. 740, pop. 764) *12 m.* NW. of Chillicothe on US 35, was the Shawnee Indian town of Chillicothe. In 1772, a Baptist minister by the name of David Jones came here to try to "save" the Indians. He found an Englishman and his wife living in the village and they helped him by trying to teach him the Shawnee language. Jones attempted to translate the Bible into Shawnese, but despite all his effort he got no response from the Indians. He finally left the territory.

After the Indians had been disbanded and forced to go farther west, the whites settled where the Indian town had been. John McNeil platted the town and called it Old Town. Later Holland Dutch settlers came in and renamed it Frankfort. The village was incorporated in 1827.

There are four churches, two Methodist Episcopal, one for colored residents, a Presbyterian Church and St. Joseph's Mission, a Catholic Church.

A grade and a high school are located in the town. The Southeastern Bus Line stops here, and a branch of the Baltimore and Ohio makes a stop to take both passengers and farm produce. The town is in an agricultural section raising corn and small grains and includes several sizeable orchards.

FRUITDALE—(alt. 863, pop. 75) *23 m.* W. of Chillicothe on ST 41, got its name from the numerous orchards in the neighborhood. It was settled in 1850 surrounding the Bethesda Church. In 1878 the town was made a stop station for the Detroit, Toledo and Ironton Railroad.

GREENLAND—(alt. 837, pop. 75) *4 m.* NE. of Frankfort at the junction of the Westfall and Egypt roads, was named by officials of the Baltimore and Ohio Railroad when a branch line was built through it.

HALLSVILLE—(alt. 841, pop. 300) *13 m.* NE. of Chillicothe on ST 180.

The first settlement on this spot was made by John Burchwalter, Ephriam Dreisbach and Ambrose Grafton. These German settlers came to Ohio in 1844 from Pennsylvania and named the new Ohio town, Economy, after the Pennsylvania town they had left. The first log cabin school was built in 1827. The Evangelical association and Methodists joined in building a church in 1844.

Today Hallsville, named after its first postmaster, has two churches, the Methodist Episcopal and the United Brethren. Hallsville children are taken in buses to the Centralia centralized school.

HIGBY—(alt. 578, pop. 10) *12 m.* S. of Chillicothe on the Higby and Waverly road, was named in honor of the first settler, Judiah Ellsworth Higby who came here in 1820, by officials of the Norfolk and Western Railroad.

HOPETOWN—(alt. 647, pop. 33) *4 m.* N. of Chillicothe on US 23.

Henry Musselman built a log grist mill here on the banks of the Scioto and named it Hope. Later, after the Norfolk & Western Railroad passed along the eastern border of the town, the name was lengthened to Hopetown. It is a cluster of houses around the general store and garage.

HUMBOLDT—(alt. 798, pop. 30) *34 m. SW. of Chillicothe, through Bainbridge and N. on ST 41.*

In 1878, the Detroit, Toledo & Ironton Railroad made a stop here and a village came into existence. It was named "Spout Springs" because of a spouting spring in the neighborhood. When the post office was established a few years later, the name was changed to the more dignified Humboldt. The post office has been discontinued.

KINGSTON—(alt. 774, pop. 857) *10 m. N. of Chillicothe on ST 159.*

The town was laid out in the early 1800's by Thomas Ing, a tailor, who named it Ingtown. In 1816 the name was changed to the more euphonious Kingston. It was incorporated in 1834 by special act of the Legislature.

Kingston was on the old Lancaster road, in the early days one of the most important thoroughfares from the south and southwest to Washington.

Widow Susanna McCutcheon kept the tavern and livery stable where the stage coaches frequently stopped. The widow played hostess to Henry Clay, Thomas Marshall and ex-President Santa Ana of Mexico. In 1817, President Monroe stopped to have dinner with Mrs. McCutcheon.

The first school was opened in 1816 and four years later the post office was established. The Presbyterian church was founded in 1798 and the Methodist Episcopal church in 1829.

The Norfolk & Western Railroad and the Valley Public Service Co. buses, both serve as transport facilities to or from the town.

Kingston serves the surrounding agricultural community both in marketing facilities and banking.

KINNIKINNICK—(alt. 700, pop. 75) *6 m. N. of Chillicothe on ST 180,* was named for Kinnikinnick Creek and the creek was named for a kind of bark found on trees along its banks that the Indians used for smoking and called Kinnikinnick.

This creek was the source of water power for many of the early mills. Among others, Mr. William McCoy built a grist mill on its bank in 1798 which was known later as Crouse's mill. David Crouse started the first paper mill on this creek in 1810. Hezekiah and Isaiah Ingham leased the mill, completed the building, and made paper until their lease expired in 1818.

LATTAVILLE—(alt. 899, pop. 50) *12 m. W. of Chillicothe on ST 28,* is named for the first settler on this site. There is a Methodist Episcopal church in the town. The general store furnished the focal point of social and economic life and the houses of the community are centered around it.

LONDONDERRY—(alt. 685, pop. 310) *13 m. E. of Chillicothe on US 50.*

This town has many names. It was platted by Adam Stewart, an Irishman, and Nathan Cox. Stewart called the town Londonderry, after his home in Ireland, but Cox and Stewart each assumed ownership of half the town, thereby leading to confusion.

In 1835, the northern half belonging to Cox was given a post office and called Schooleys after the first postmaster. A little later, when Cox sold his half to Stewart, the post office was moved to the south end of the town and called Gillespieville after its postmaster. In more recent days the residents reverted to the original name, although the town is commonly called "Derry", an abbreviation of the whole name. The town has two churches, a Methodist Episcopal church and a Friends Meeting House. The B. & O. Railroad station serving Londonderry is at Vigo, a mile and a quarter away.

LYNDON—(alt. 915, pop. 125) *18.5 m.* W. of Chillicothe on ST 28.

The town was laid out in 1853 by John E. Huggins who named it Zora. A few years later the land came into the possession of a family named Langdon and was named Lyndon after their home town in Massachusetts.

There is one church in Lyndon, called Holiness, where separate services are held for the white and colored congregation. The Buckeye Stages Bus Line and the Baltimore & Ohio Railroad pass through the town.

MASSIEVILLE—(alt. 600, pop. 200) *5 m.* S. of Chillicothe on US 23.

Waller Massie built a sawmill here in 1852 and the village developed around it. The village was known as Waller until 1868 when the post office was established and the name was changed to Massieville. Today the town is strung along route 23 with very little prospects of further growth.

There are three churches in the town, the Methodist Episcopal, Holiness, and colored Baptist. Smaller children go to one of the four one-room schools in the village. High school students go by bus to the Centralia centralized school.

MOORESVILLE—(alt. 680, pop. 20) *6 m.* E. of Chillicothe on the Charleston pike near the junction on Walnut and Little Walnut Creeks, is said to have been settled as early as 1800 by a family named Moore from the south of Ireland.

NIPGEN—(alt. 1,075, pop. 80) *15 m.* SW. of Chillicothe on the Huntington pike.

The town was first called Coopersville, possibly after a small cooper shop which may have existed there at some time. It was renamed Nipgen in honor of John A. Nipgen of Chillicothe in 1896. There are two churches, the Methodist and Church of Christ. The town was once known as Possum Trot.

RICHMONDALE—(alt. 592, pop. 215) *13 m.* SE. of Chillicothe on US 35

The town was platted around 1811 and called Moffittstown after a Mr. Moffitts who had built a grist mill here at the junction of the Scioto and Salt Creek.

It was settled by Meekers, Strattons and Minears from Connecticut and later called Richmond. When the post office was established it was renamed Richmondale to avoid confusing it with another town of the same name. It soon had a tavern and a blacksmith shop.

Indian graves nearby bear witness to previous occupation. When the graves were opened some years ago, crude lead balls, charcoal and animal bones were found.

Salt Creek in the vicinity is very popular for fishing.

ROXABELL—(alt. 732, pop. 250) *13 m.* W. of Chillicothe on the Frankfort-Lattaville road, was founded in 1875 and started as a flourishing railroad town, for shipping livestock and farm produce. It is no longer an important railroad junction. Its population has decreased and the business section is composed of two general stores with gasoline pumps in front. The population is almost equally divided between colored and white residents.

There are two Baptist Churches, one of them colored.

SOUTH SALEM—(alt. 912, pop. 201) *19.5 m.* W. of Chillicothe along Buckskin Creek, just off ST 28, turning S. at Lyndon, was settled around 1800, and in 1802 a Presbyterian church was built. Impetus was given to the town when the South Salem Academy for boys was opened under James S. Fullerton and John Huston in 1842. The community of South Salem was laid out in 1846, by John Sample to provide board and lodging for students, faculty and visiting parents at the Academy. The Academy apparently existed until near Civil War times.

The town has three churches, Presbyterian, Methodist and Baptist.

SPARGURSVILLE—(alt. 709, pop. 25) *12 m.* SW. of Chillicothe on the Bourneville-Nipgen road.

The town was settled in 1875 and named after one of the first settlers. A mill was built in 1890. The town has a general store, a lumber yard, and two churches, Christian and Church of Christ. The Detroit, Toledo & Ironton Railroad passes through the village.

STORMS—(alt. 724, pop. 20) *11 m.* SW. of Chillicothe on the edge of the Paint Creek Valley, was founded in 1802 and named for an early settler, Peter Storms. At one time Storms was an important shipping center for lumber and grain. It is still a station on the railroad.

SUMMIT HILL—(alt. 1,085, pop. 40) *14 m.* SW. of Chillicothe on the Huntington Pike, was first settled in 1875 as a station of the Detroit, Toledo and Ironton Railroad. It is in the hilliest section of the county and was named for Summit Hill, to the east, 1,320 ft. above sea level. Hatfield Knob with 1,224 feet elevation and Horseback Knob with 1,341 feet elevation are nearby.

THRIFTON—(alt. 750, pop. 25) *22.5 m.* W. of Chillicothe, near ST 41 at the edge of Greenfield in Highland county.

Thrifton was started as a railroad camp when the Detroit, Toledo & Ironton was being built. When the camp was dismantelled, the small settlement survived.

TUCSON—(alt. 724, pop. 50) *8 m.* NE. of Chillicothe on the Charleston Pike along Walnut Creek grew up around a small grist mill about 1800.

VIGO—(alt. 617, pop. 150) *12 m.* SE. of Chillicothe on US 35 is a small railroad terminal adjacent to Londonderry. It is served by the Londonderry post office.

YELLOWBUD—(alt. 670, pop. 200) *12 m.* N. of Chillicothe on ST 104, had its beginnings in 1802 when a grist mill was built on Yellowbud creek by Francis and Baylis Nichols.

In canal days, Yellowbud was one of the most important port towns and shipping centers. It was laid out as a village in 1845 by Isaiah Ingham, John

Boggs and Samuel G. Lutz when it was already a thriving community. Joshua Clark of Lancaster had built a distillery in 1835 and there was a sizeable pork packing business, a grist mill and several stores.

The first dry-dock on the eastern division of the canal, for the construction and repair of canal boats, was built here in 1837.

With the passing of the canal, Yellowbud's heyday was over. There is still a grain elevator in the town and today it is a picturesque community in the deep valley of Yellowbud creek.

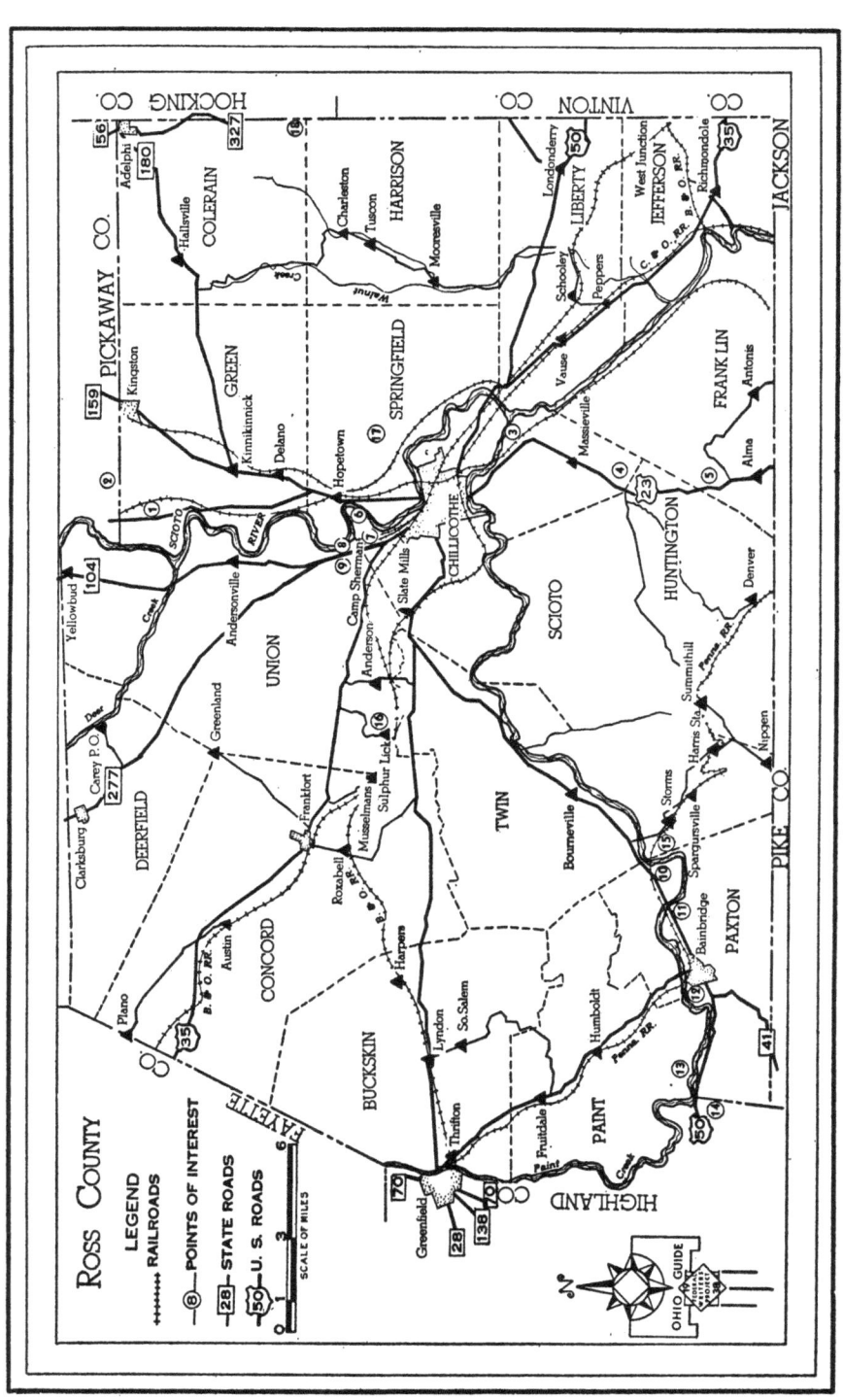

POINTS OF INTEREST IN THE COUNTY

US 23—N. from Chillicothe

1. CATHERINE COUGAR MONUMENT, 8.5 m. N. of Chillicothe on US 23, (R) was erected to the memory of Catherine Cougar Goodman, held captive here by the Shawnee Indians for five years, from 1744 to 1749. Mrs. Goodman recognized the locality of her captive days when she came to live in Chillicothe in 1798.

2. IN LOGAN ELM STATE PARK, 13 m. NE. of Chillicothe on US 23 and 1 m. R. on ST 361, is the tree under which Logan, famous Indian chief, responded to Lord Dunmore around 1774. When he was summoned to a conference between the Indians and whites, Logan did not attend and Dunmore sent a trader, John Gibson, to find the reason. Logan's answer is one of the most famous speeches in American history and all sympathy goes to this lonely Indian betrayed by the white man.

It follows: "I appeal to any white man to say if ever he entered Logan's cabin hungry and he gave him not meat; if ever he came cold and naked and he clothed him not.

"During the course of the last long and bloody war, Logan remained idle in his cabin and advocated peace. Such was my love for the whites, that my countrymen pointed as they passed and said, 'Logan is the friend of the white man'. I had even thought to have lived with you, but for the injuries of one man. Colonel Cresap, the last spring, in cold blood and unprovoked, murdered all the relatives of Logan not even sparing my women and children. There runs not a drop of my blood in the veins of any living creature. This called on me for revenge. I have sought it. I have killed many. I have fully glutted my vengeance. For my country, I rejoice at the beams of peace. But do not harbor a thought that mine is the joy of fear. Logan never felt fear. He will not turn on his heel to save his life. Who is there to mourn Logan? No one."

US 23 S. from Chillicothe

3. FELIX RENICK STATE PARK, 2 m. S. of Chillicothe, on US 23 (L), is the smallest State park consisting of a few square feet around a marker establishing the location of the first sale of Shorthorn cattle in the United States. This land was once a part of the Renick farm.

4. OBSERVATION TOWER—*(open for picnicking)* 9 m. S. of Chillicothe US 23, L. on crest of the hill, is situated in the Scioto Trail Forest. Camp Stony Creek, of the Civilian Conservation Corp is located here.

5. HEWITT'S CAVE, 11 m. S. of Chillicothe, on US 23, (L) was the home of a hermit, William Hewitt, for 14 years. Hewitt was a Virginian, but because of some quarrel with his family had come west. He hunted along the Kanawha River for several years and then came to Ross County where he lived until his death in 1834 at the age of 70.

He was a good hunter and a familiar figure to the settlers, clad in his buckskin and fur. During the summer he usually spent several weeks at Fruit Hill, home of Duncan McArthur, paying for this hospitality in game. His obituary is inscribed on the shelf of the cave.

ST 104 N. of Chillicothe

6. CAMP SHERMAN, *1.5 m.* NW. of Chillicothe on ST 104 and US 35, was a huge military city during the World War. A few frame buildings are all that is left of the camp.

7. UNITED STATES INDUSTRIAL REFORMATORY — *(no visitors)* 2 m. NW. of Chillicothe on ST 104.

Shortly after the War, Congress authorized the Attorney General, the Secretary of War, and the Secretary of the Interior to select a site for an industrial reformatory to be used for the confinement of men between seventeen and thirty years of age who have been convicted of offense against the United States Government. The site selected was a portion of the land that had been Camp Sherman and for a time some of the old wartime barracks were used to house the prisoners.

In 1932, money was appropriated to construct modern fireproof buildings so that now the 1,500 inmates of this institution are housed in modern structures.

Wire fence has taken the place of old fashioned high stone walls and the prisoners are regulated by an honor system. Schools are maintained and the men are taught various trades, including farming and dairying.

8. MOUND CITY—3 m. W. of Chillicothe on ST 104, with its 24 mounds was leveled when the field became part of the army encampment. The mounds have since been reconstructed from accurate measurements taken before the war. The park surrounding Mound City has been improved under the Works Project Administration and a shelter house erected. *(SEE THE VALLEY OF THE MOUND BUILDERS.)*

9. THE UNITED STATES VETERANS' ADMINISTRATION HOSPITAL, *5 m.* N. of Chillicothe on ST 104 (L), was built in 1924 and is also located on Camp Sherman territory. Three more buildings were added in 1929 and 1932 and two more are planned. The hospital houses 1,446 patients suffering from nervous and mental disorders, at the present time.

Occupational therapy is used as a method of treatment here and includes, poultry raising, stock raising and farming. Approximately 365 persons are employed at this institution, including physicians, nurses, attendants and others.

US 50 SW from Chillicothe

10. SEIP MOUND STATE PARK—*14 m.* SW. of Chillicothe on US 50, (R) is part of the Seip works excavated by Dr. William Mills of the Ohio Archeological and Historical Society. *(SEE THE VALLEY OF THE MOUND BUILDERS.)*

11. SITE OF THE LAST INDIAN FIGHT IN THE SCIOTO VALLEY —*16 m.* SW. of Chillicothe on US 50 (L) *1 m.* W. of Seip Mound and *.05 m.* S. of Paint Creek where Nathaniel Massie and his party met the Shawnee chieftain John and his braves. *(SEE SHAWNEE AND PIONEER.)*

12. FALLS OF PAINT CREEK, *19 m.* W. of Chillicothe on US 50, *1 m.* N. on ST 41 and *1 m.* W. on first side road (L), was once the site of the town of New Amsterdam, abandoned with the founding of Bainbridge. The creek

is about 40 feet wide at this point, and the falls average from four to five feet in height.

13. RAPID FORGE, *1 m.* above Falls of Paint Creek, is the site of a dam and race built by William James, John Woodbridge, and William Keys Bond in 1815. In 1817, Mr. James and the Woodbridge brothers of Chillicothe joined in partnership and built a forge equipped with four power hammers and four coal blast furnaces. The charcoal needed for operation came from the surrounding forests, but the ore was brought from near West Union by wagon. The iron produced here was taken by wagon to Chillicothe and to Manchester. Nails and tires were manufactured around 1830 and were of such an excellent quality that they commanded a very high price. Bond and James sold their interests to John Woodbridge. About the middle 60's Rapid Forge was forced out of existence by the competition of larger foundaries with more modern equipment.

14. THE SEVEN CAVES, *(open, adm. 50c)* 23 *m.* W. of Chillicothe on US 50 just over the boundary line of Ross County in Highland County, are located in a 110 acre park. There are three nature trails: the Cave Canyon Trail, the Palisades Trail, and the Indian Trail.

The Cave Canyon Trail winds past five of the caves. They are: Witches Cave, Cave of the Springs, Phantom Cave, Dancing Cave and Bear Cave.

The Palisades Trail begins at a lofty point overlooking Rocky Fork Creek which abounds in small-mouthed bass, rock bass, crappies and catfish. Palisades 100 feet high reveal the Rocky Fork Gorge.

The Indian Trail winds through Et-Nah Woods, the site of an Indian village where Johnny Appleseed later planted an orchard. The stump of an old apple tree, to which Daniel Boone was once tied as a captive, is near the site of the town.

Trees and flowers have been identified along the nature trails. The caves are lighted by electricity. There are camping, swimming and fishing facilities.

15. COPPERAS MOUNTAIN, *16 m.* SW. of Chillicothe on US 50, *4.5 m.* from Bourneville on the Jones Levee Road, bears a resemblance to the bad lands in the West. The cliff along Paint Creek, is about 75 feet high and deep gulleys have been cut through the shale and sandstone concretions. There is some sulphate of iron or copperas between the layers of shale and at one time the cliff was worked for copperas but such a small amount was obtained that the project was abandoned.

US 35 SE of Chillicothe

16. SULPHUR LICK SPRINGS, 7 *m.* W. of Chillicothe on US 35 (L) 2 *m.* on Sulphur Lick Road, was once the site of an Indian village and the Springs were called "Great Medicine Waters". There is a hotel here today which at one time was quite a fashionable resort. The Spring water contains Sulphate-Magnesium, Sulphate of Calcium and Chloride of Sodium and is considered to have medicinal value.

17. MOUNT LOGAN STATE FOREST, 2 *m.* E of Chillicothe on the Marietta Pike, covers 400 acres of wooded lands. The series of hills, including

Mount Logan, was the source of the seal of Ohio. Mount Logan was once the hideaway of the Indian Chief Logan.

18. ROSS-HOCKING PROJECT CAMP, *(open)* was constructed under the Works Project Administration in Ohio. The camp lies chiefly in Ross County and extends into Hocking County. It lies in a section previously known as Tar Hollow, long the home of squatters who existed chiefly through the manufacture and sale of "moonshine".

The camp has four groups of sleeping cabins composed of seven cabins each, recreation-dining hall and kitchen, infirmary, cook's quarters. Situated on an 18 acre lake, the camp provides bathing and boating facilities. There are nature trails, shelter houses, picnic furnaces and tables surrounding the camp.

—*Ireland*

CITY AND COUNTY CHRONOLOGY

1796—Nathaniel Massie founded Chillicothe.

1798—Ross County was formed by proclamation of Governor St. Clair.

1803—The State of Ohio came into existence and Chillicothe was its capital.

1810—State Capital moved to Zanesville for two years and then moved back to Chillicothe until 1816 when it was permanently located in Columbus.

1831—The Ohio Erie Canal was completed from Cleveland through Chillicothe.

1838—Chillicothe was given a city charter by the State Legislature and had a population of 5,000.

1845—A Branch of the State Bank was organized in Chillicothe.

1849—A statewide cholera epidemic spread to Chillicothe. Prayer and fasting were observed by proclamation of the Governor throughout Ross County.

1852—Fire destroyed one fourth of Chillicothe property along Water Street.

1858—Engineers, firemen and brakemen on the Marietta and Cincinnati Railroad struck for a regular pay period in the first strike to occur in the County.

1870—Floods damaged town property and washed out bridges, roads, fences and buildings in the County.

1877—The first telephone was installed in Chillicothe.

1888—Free delivery of mail was inaugurated in Chillicothe.

1896—Chillicothe celebrated its centennial.

1900—Chillicothe had a population of 12,975.

1903—The celebration of the centennial of the State of Ohio was held in Chillicothe.

1913—The worst flood in the history of Ross County completely tied up all transportation, utilities and industry.

1917—Camp Sherman, huge mobilization camp during the World War, was constructed.

1926—Pricer Mound of the Seip Group was explored by Professor H. C. Shetrone of the Ohio Historical and Archeological Society.

1930—Drought ruined Ross County crops.

BIBLIOGRAPHY

Bennett, Henry Holcomb. *State Centennial History,* Selwyn A. Brant, Madison, Wisconsin, 1902.

Evans, Lyle S. *History of Ross County,* Vols. 1 and 2, Lewis Publishing Co., Chicago, Illinois, 1917.

Frary, I. T., *Early Homes of Ohio,* Garrett and Massie Inc., Richmond, Va., 1936.

Fowke, Gerald. *Archeological History of Ohio,* Fred Heer Printing Co., Columbus, Ohio, 1902.

Galbreath, Charles B., *History of Ohio,* American Historical Society, Inc., Chicago and New York City, 1925.

Gist, Christopher. *Journal (1750-51),* W. M. Darling and J. F. Welding and Co., 1839.

Hyde, J. E. *Geology of Camp Sherman Quadrangle,* Geological Survey of Ohio, Fourth Series, Bulletin 23, Columbus, 1921.

Howe, Henry. *Historical Collections of Ohio,* published by the State of Ohio, 1908.

King, I. F. *The Coming and Going of Ohio Droving,* Ohio State Archeological and Historical Quarterly, Vol. 17, pp. 249. (1908)

Mills, William C. *Archeological Atlas of Ohio,* Ohio State Archeological and Historical Society, Columbus, Ohio, 1914.

Renick, Fullerton, Nipgen. *Che-le-co-the,* Knikerbocker Press, New York City, 1896.

Roseboom, Eugene Holloway and Weisenburger, Francis Phelps, *A History of Ohio,* Prentice-Hall Inc., New York City, 1934.

Shetrone, H. C. *Primer of Ohio Archeology,* Ohio Archeological and Historical Society.

Scott, Franklin Goddard and Ferrenz, George Hils, *The Early Architecture of Chillicothe, Ohio.* Bound Thesis, Architecture Library, Ohio State University.

Williams, Brothers, *History of Ross and Highland Counties,* Williams Bros. Publishing Co., Cleveland, Ohio, 1880.

Files: *Scioto Gazette* and *News Advertiser.*

ACKNOWLEDGEMENTS

The Ohio Writers Project wishes to express appreciation for information and advice given in the preparation of the Chillicothe and Ross County Guide by the following persons: Judge Marshall Fenton, Mr. E. S. Wenis, Mr. Lyle Evans, Mrs. Peter J. Blosser, Mr. Earl Barnhart, Mr. Martin Chandler, Mr. Gregg Wolf, Mr. Robert Segal, Mr. Junius K. Hunter, Mr. Albert Schlegel, Mr. C. J. Ware, Mr. Russell Savage, Mr. Ben Segal, Mr. Roy Drury, Mr. Walter M. Norvell, Mr. James W. Blair and Mr. William Corry.

Paper used in the Guide was furnished the Northwest Territory Committee through the courtesy of the Mead Corporation and the Chillicothe Paper Company.

Cuts used to illustrate the text were lent by the Chillicothe *News Advertiser* and represent the work of William Ireland, John Bennett, H. H. Bennett, and Dard Hunter.

The Writers' Project also wishes to thank the Ross County Historical Society and its members for their interest and suggestions.

ROSS COUNTY

IN

PICTURES

THE OLD MILLER HOUSE

— *Courtesy, Eugene Rigney, Chillicothe Camera Club*

DOORWAY, MCLANDBURG FULLERTON HOME

DOORWAYS AND GRILLE RAILINGS, ST. MARY'S CONVENT

Paint Hill, the Old George Renick Home

In the Garden at Paint Hill

THE OLD McGIRR HOUSE

SECOND STREET DOORWAY

SIDE PORCHES IN THE SOUTHERN MANNER

THE SCHILDER HOUSE

Bridge Over Deer Creek

Late Afternoon in Yellowbud

SABBATH AFTERNOON

SPRING LAMBS

Plowing in March

The Paper Companies from the Air
— *Courtesy, Mead Corp.*

WOOD WEATHERING FOR WOOD PULP, MEAD CORPORATION

MAKING PAPER, CHILLICOTHE PAPER COMPANY

MAKING SHOES

— *Courtesy, U. S. Shoe Corp.*

The U. S. Reformatory, Administration Building

U. S. Veterans' Hospital, Administration Building

CELL BLOCK, UNITED STATES REFORMATORY

DINING HALL IN VETERANS' HOSPITAL

Ross County Historical Society's Museum

SCIOTO TRAIL FOREST IN WINTER

— *Courtesy, Earl Barnhart*

Road to Bourneville — US 50

— *Courtesy, Mrs. Lincoln C. Anderson*

OAK HILL . . . R. F. D.

Paint Crossing Farm, East of Bainbridge

— *Courtesy, Mrs. Lincoln C. Anderson*

Town Pump, As It Was in the 80's

— Courtesy, Mr. Albert Schlegel

THE TOWN IN THE VALLEY FROM PAINT HILL

www.ingramcontent.com/pod-product-compliance
Lightning Source LLC
Chambersburg PA
CBHW060533080526
44586CB00012B/720